This is a work of fiction. Names, characters, places, and incidents either are the product of the author's imagination or are used fictitiously. Any resemblance to actual persons, living or dead, events, or locales is entirely coincidental.

Copyright © 2023 Beach Day Books

All rights reserved. No part of this book may be reproduced or used in any manner without written permission of the copyright owner except for the use of quotations in a book review.

First paperback edition April 2023

All illustrations by Midjourney

ISBN 979-8-3980-3461-5

Published by Beach Day Books
BeachDayBooks.com

Dedicated to all the animals of the world.

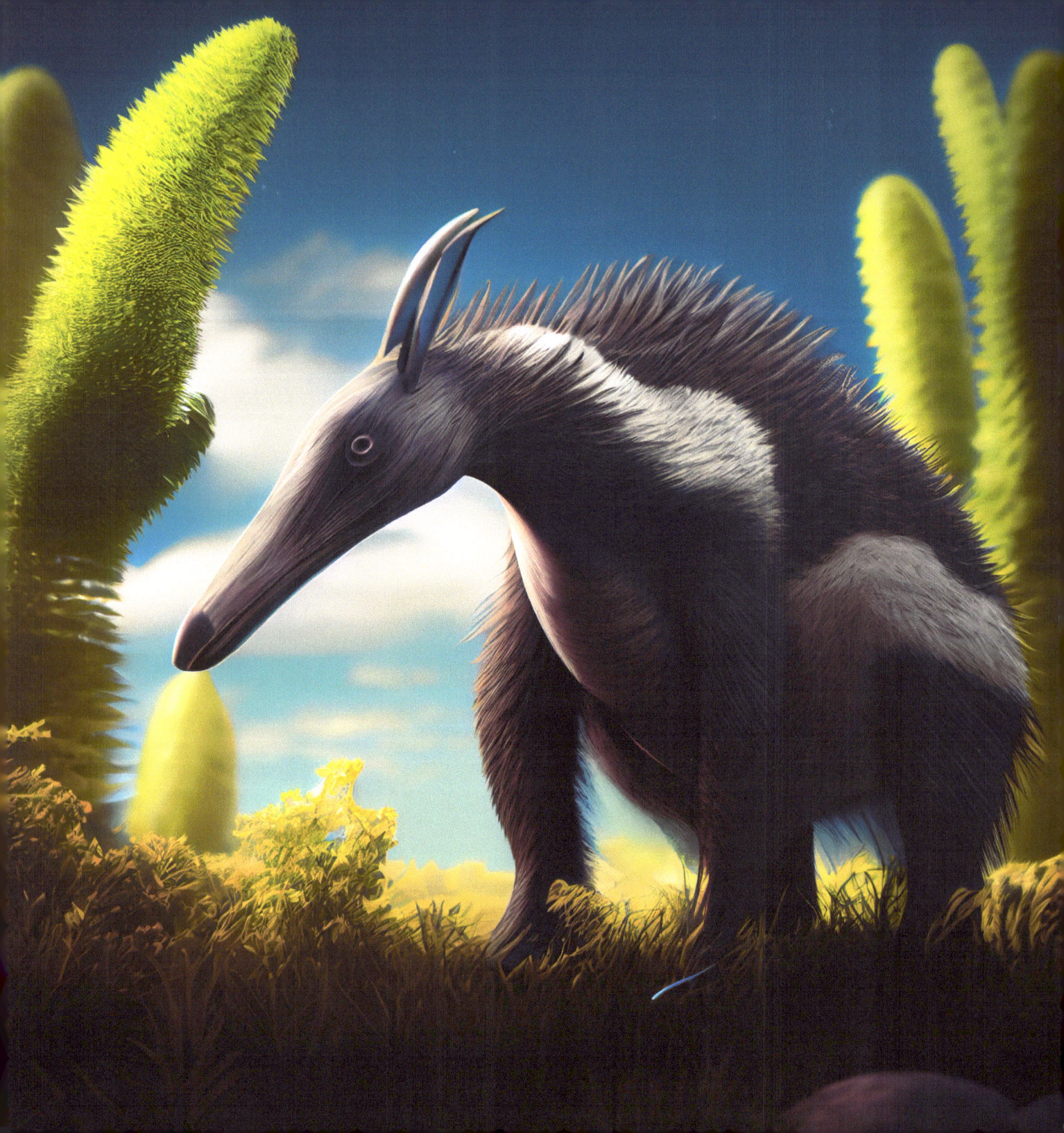

Alvin the Anteater

ate ants all day

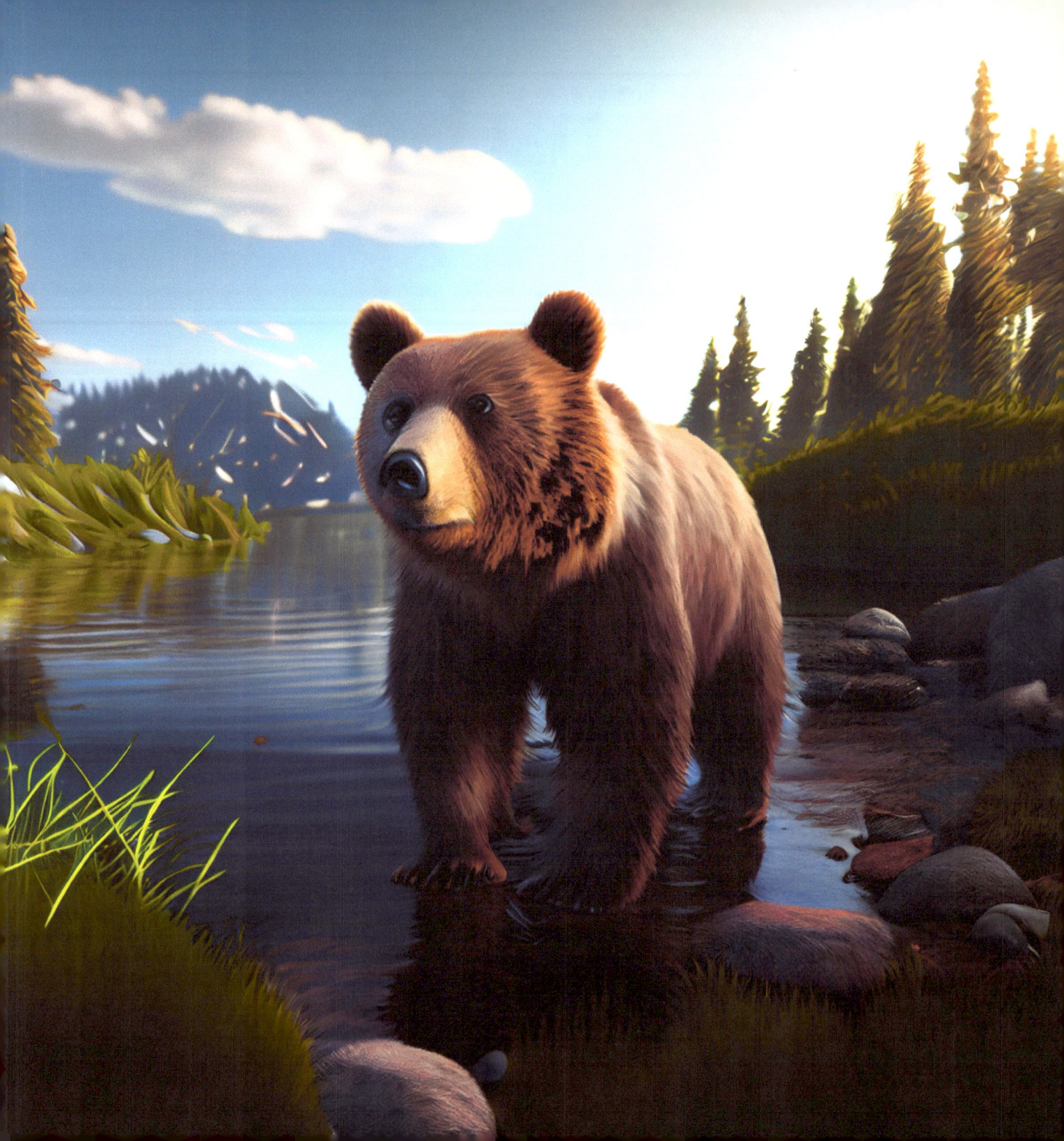

Bella the Bear

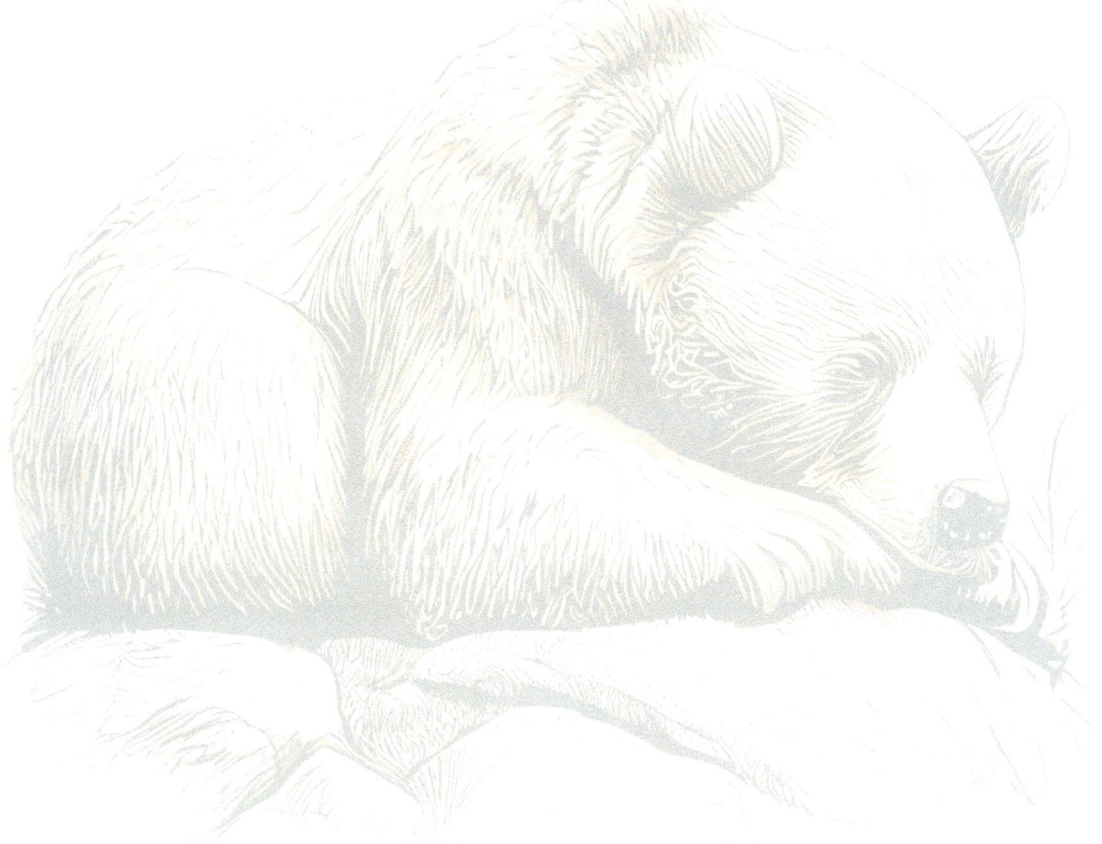

liked to sleep and play

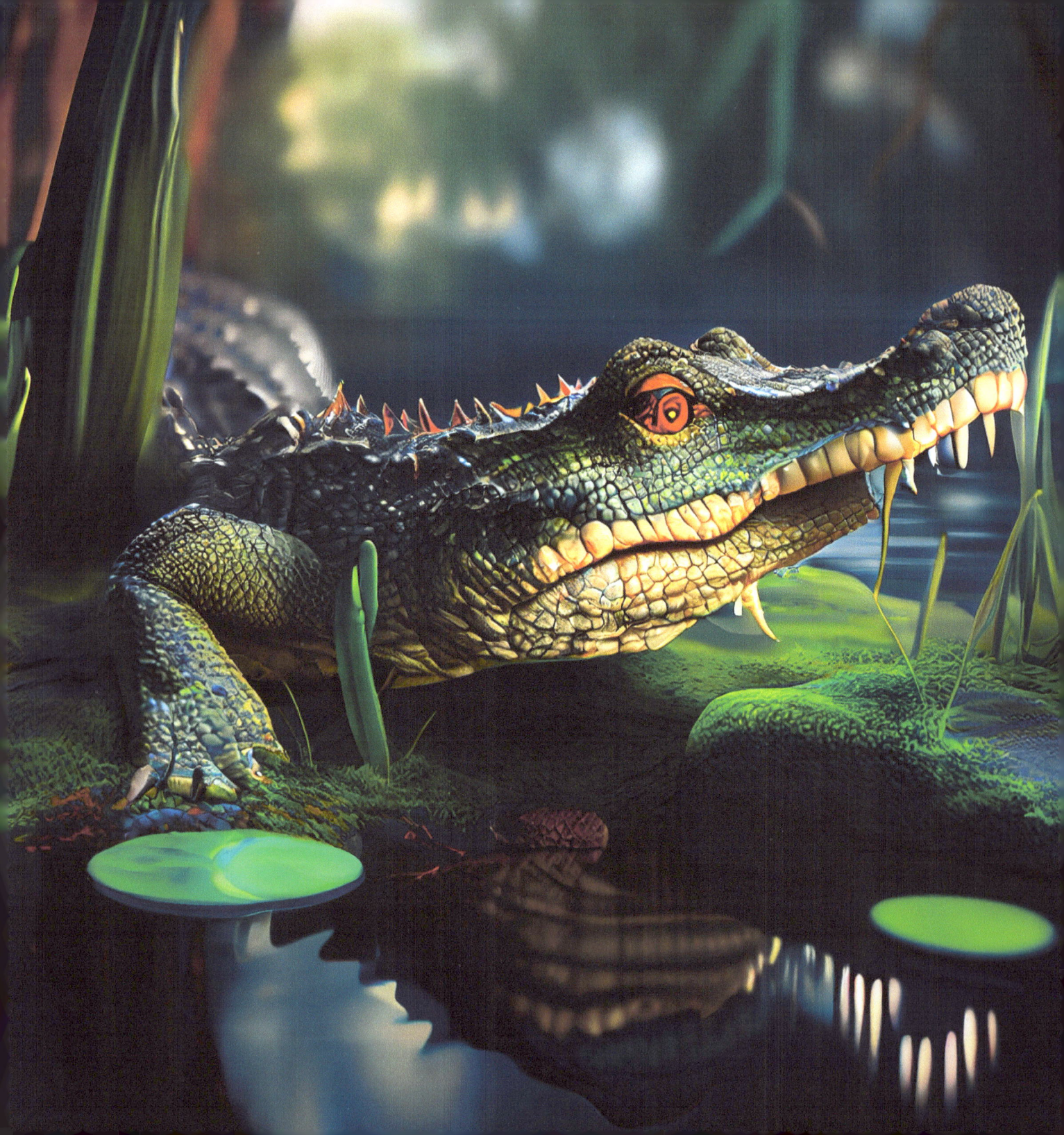

Charlie the Crocodile

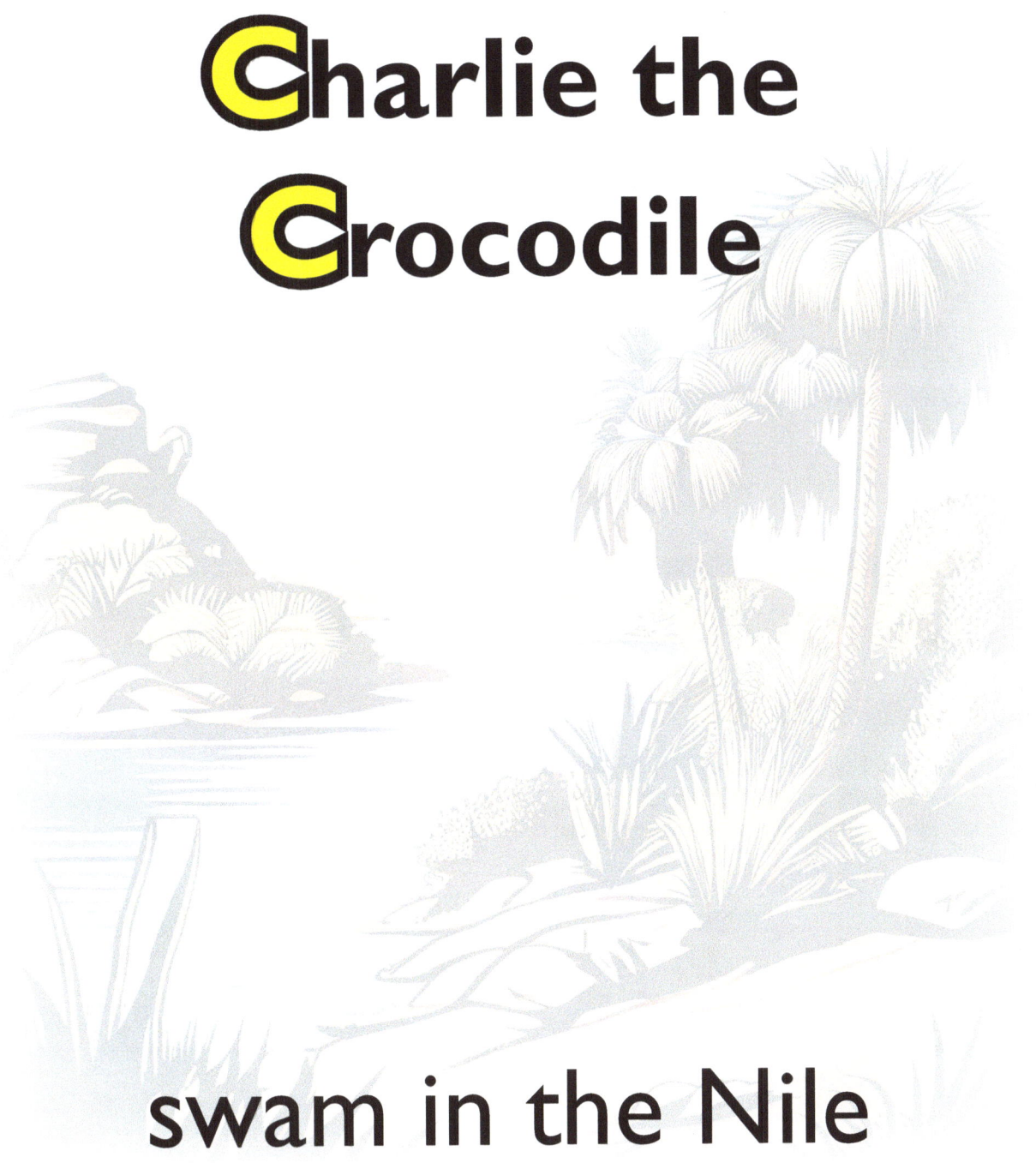

swam in the Nile

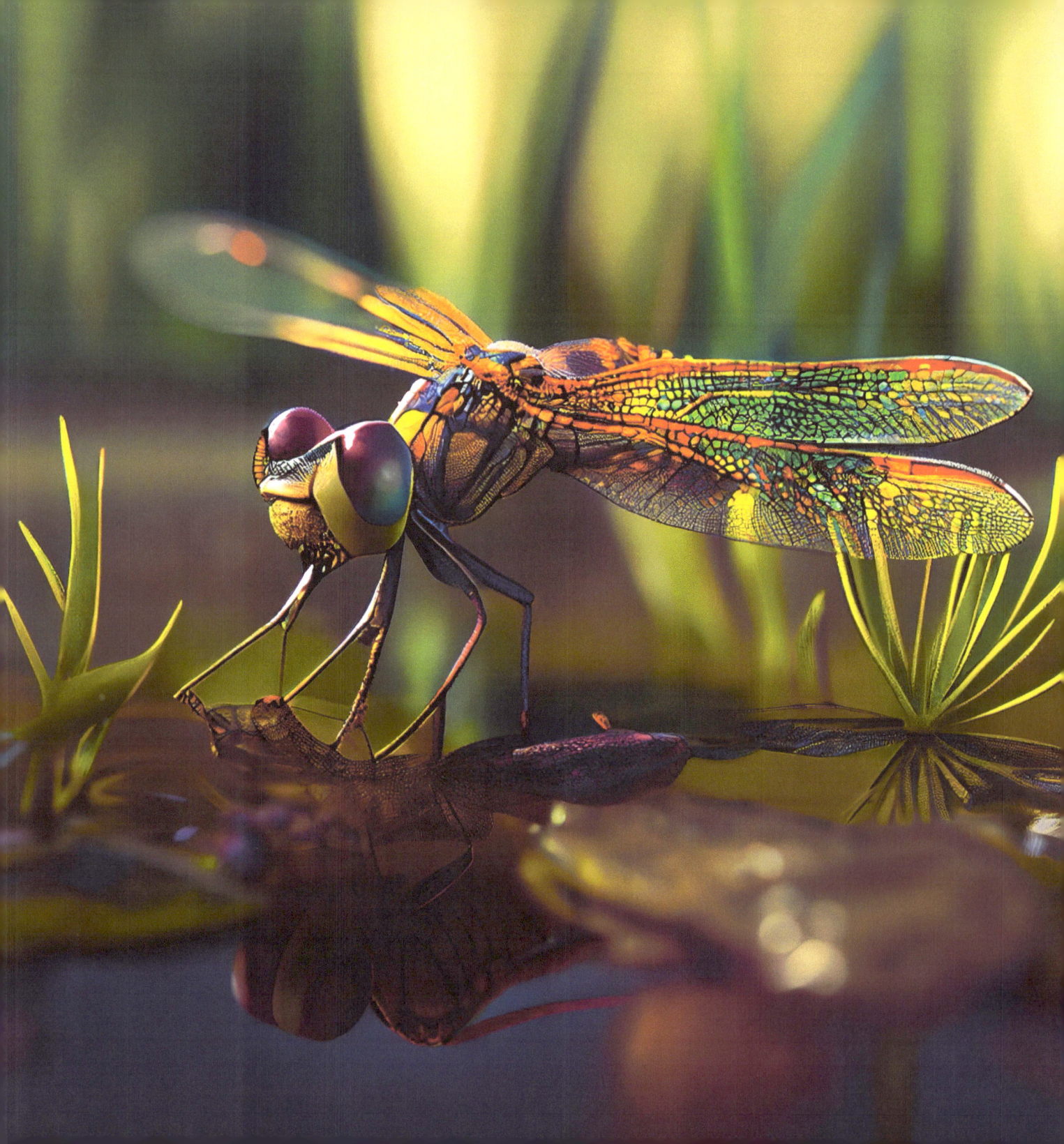

Danny the Dragonfly

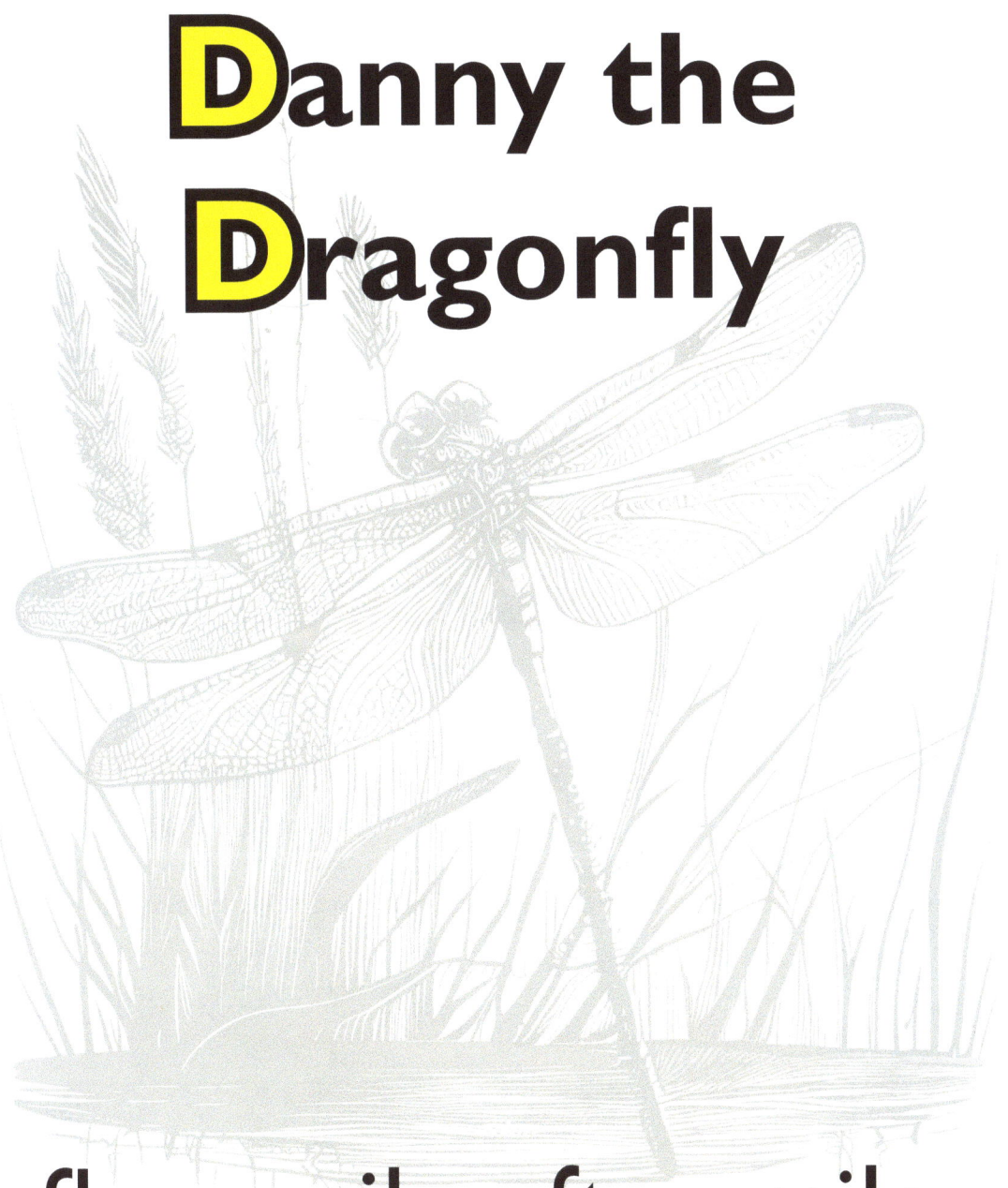

flew mile after mile

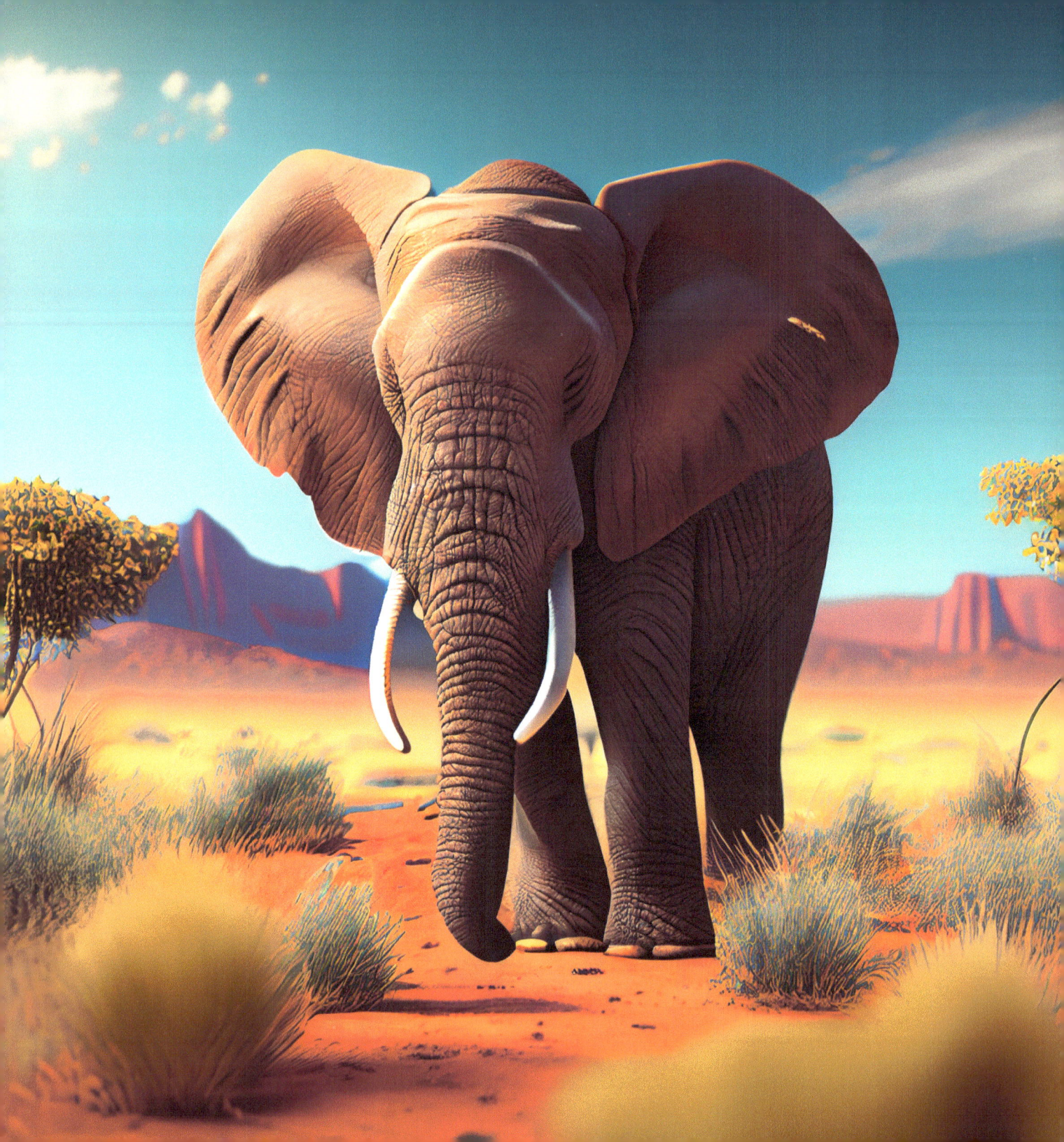

Ellie the Elephant

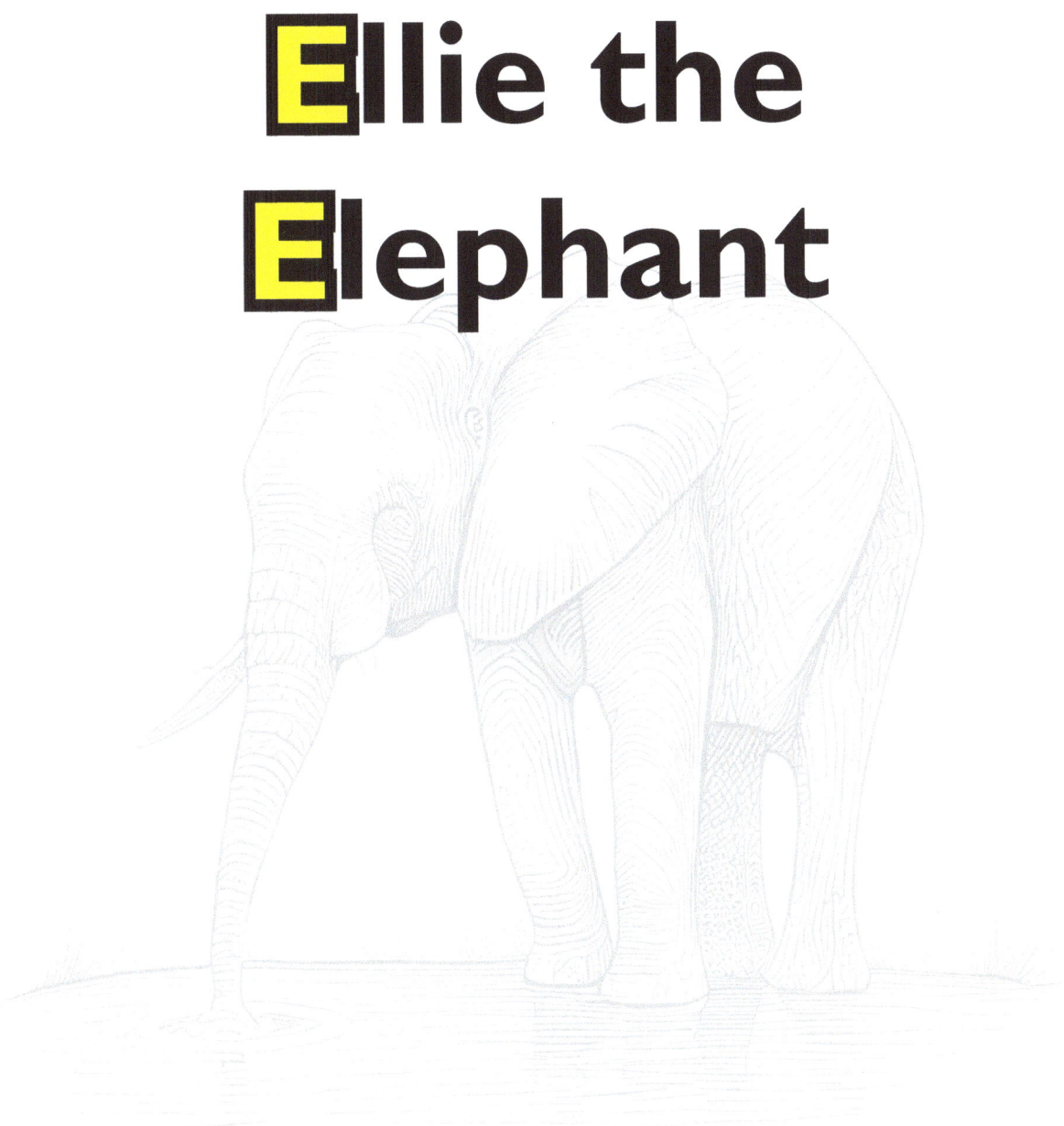

had a trunk so long

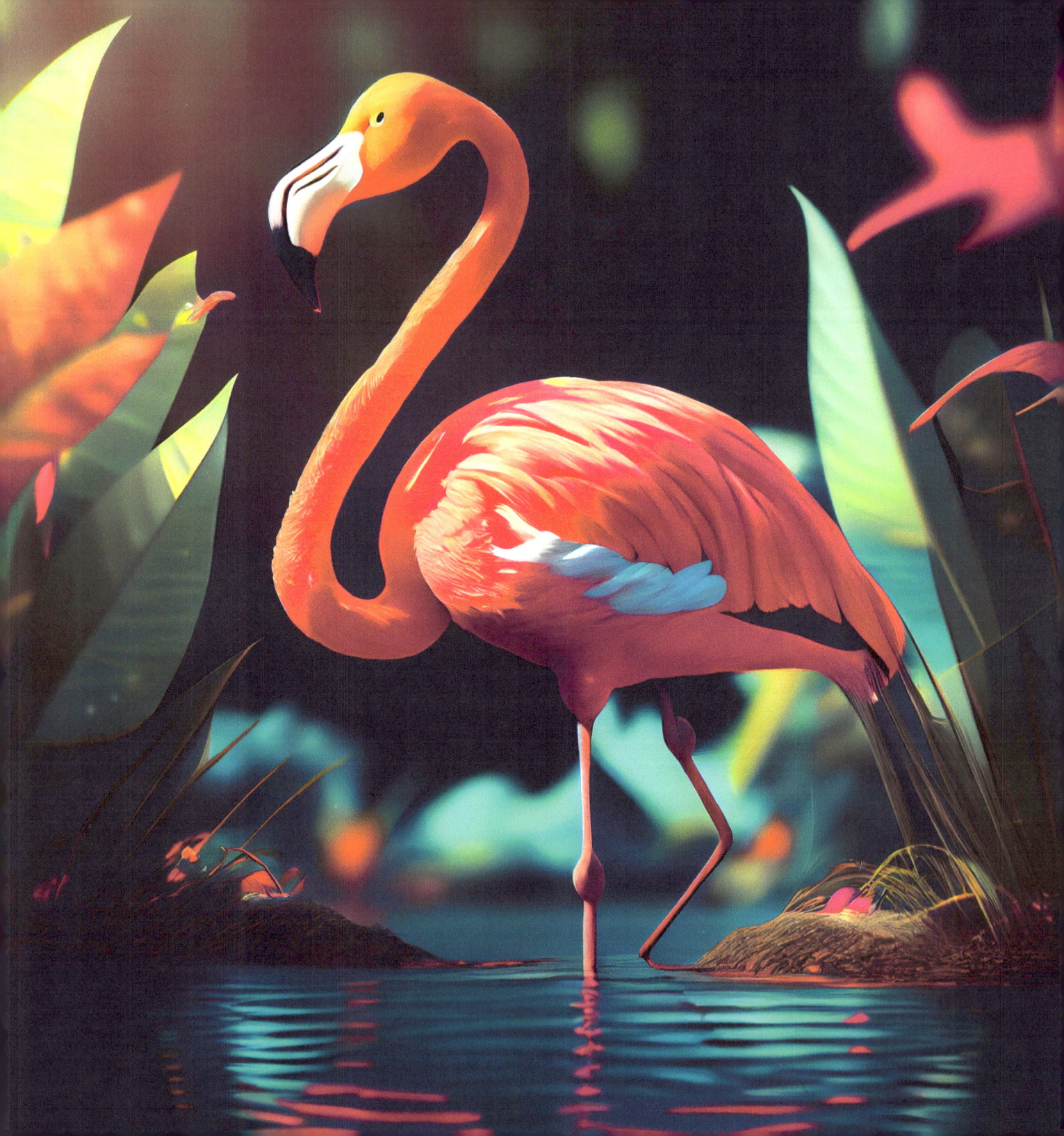

Fiona the **F**lamingo

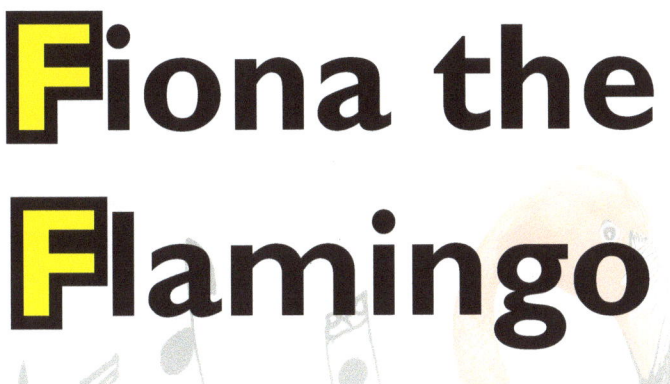

danced to her own song

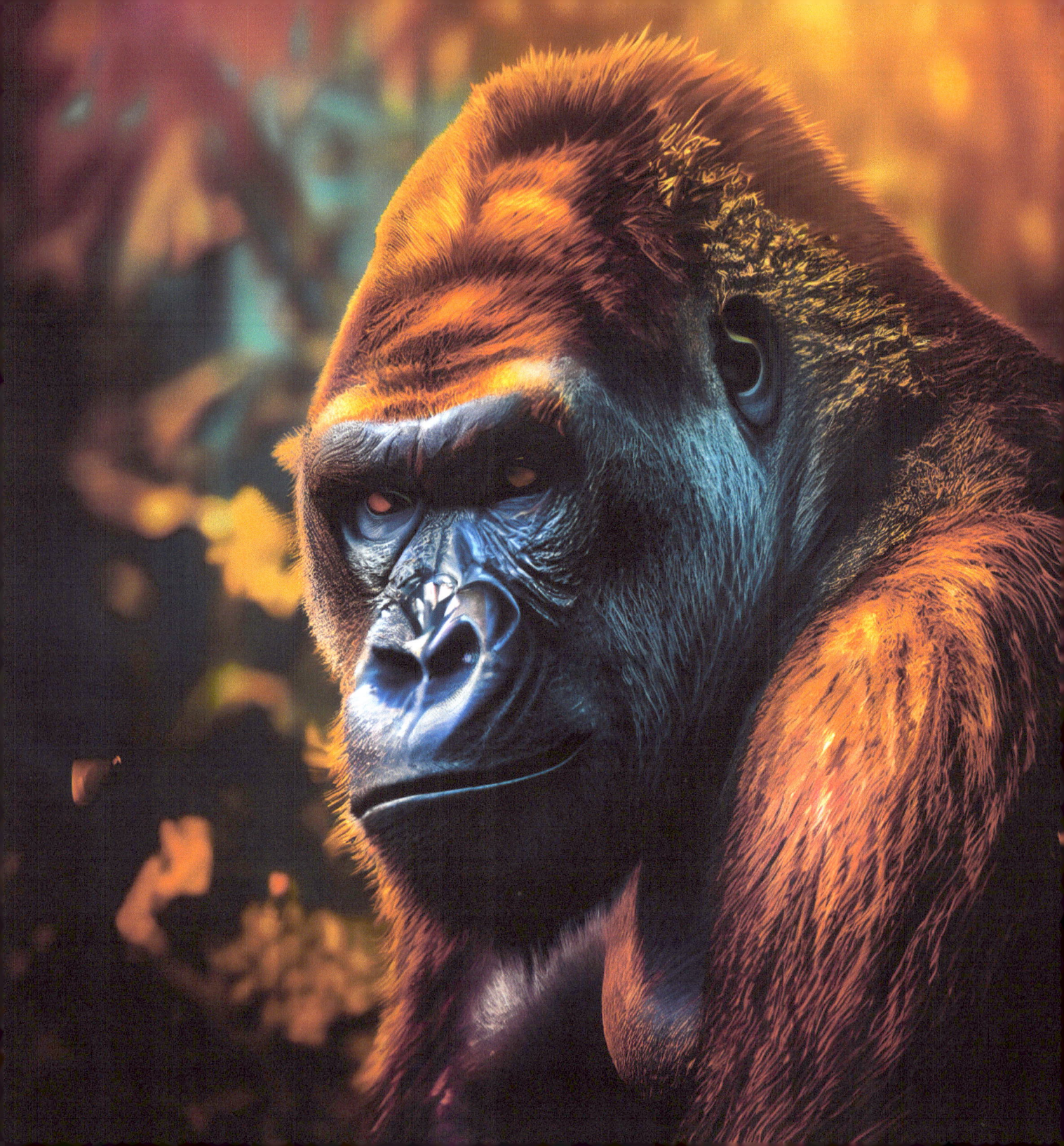

Gabe the Gorilla

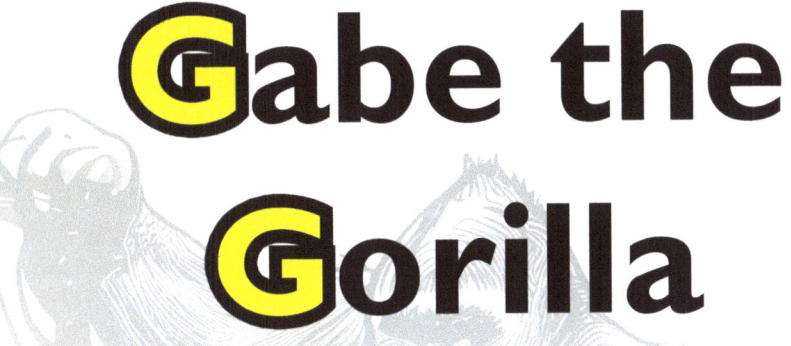

liked to climb up high

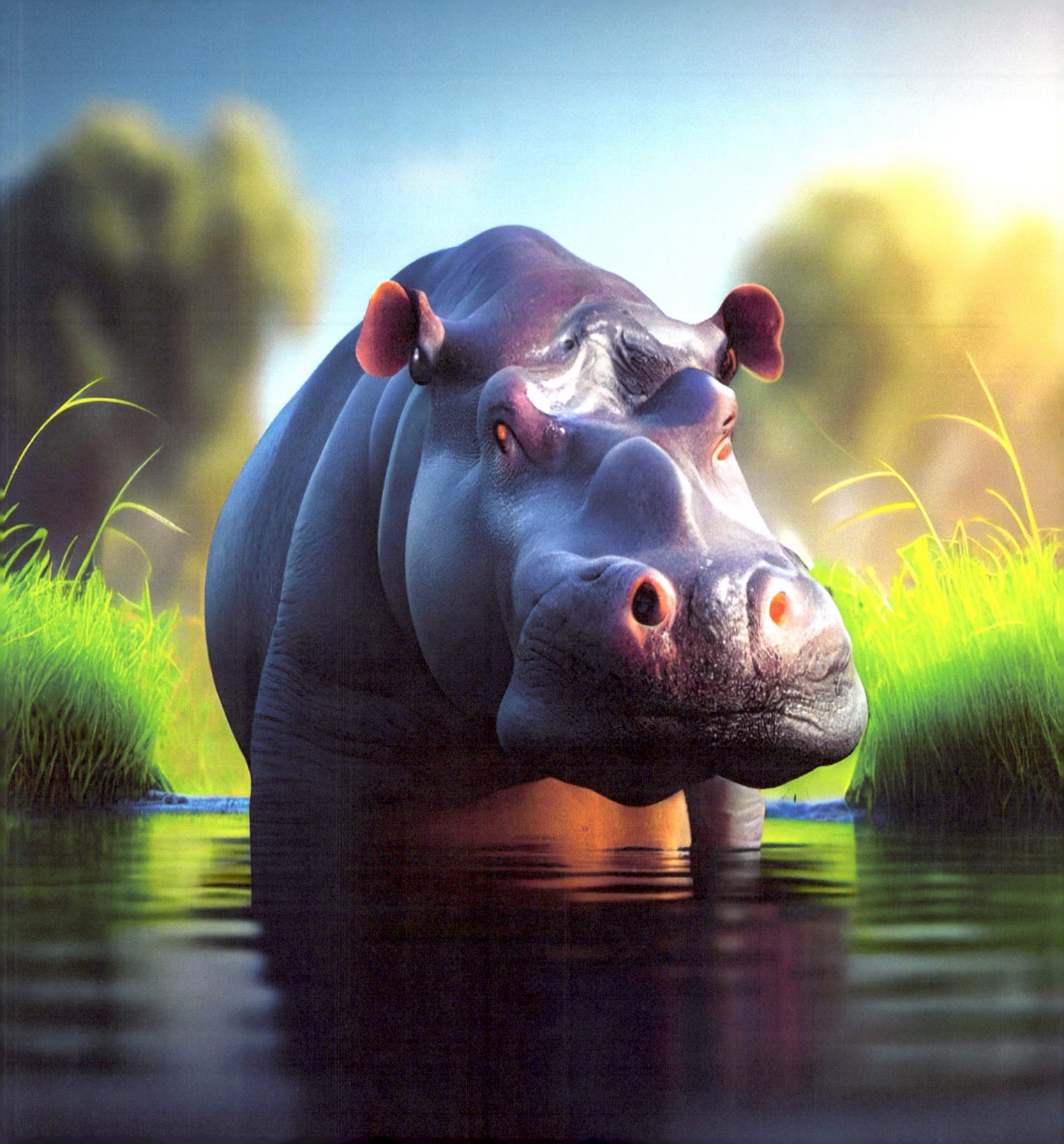

Henry the Hippo

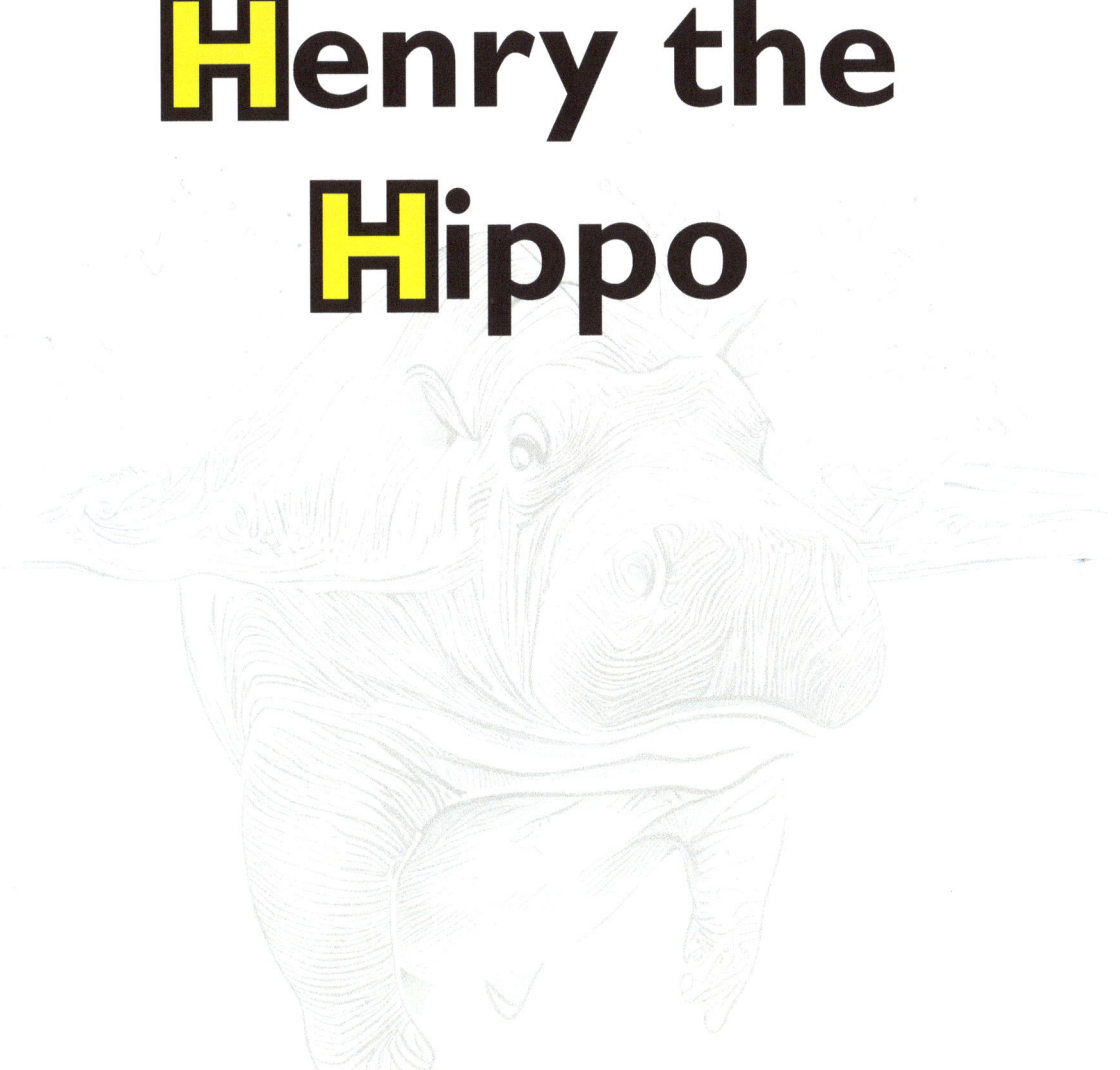

swam and splashed with a sigh

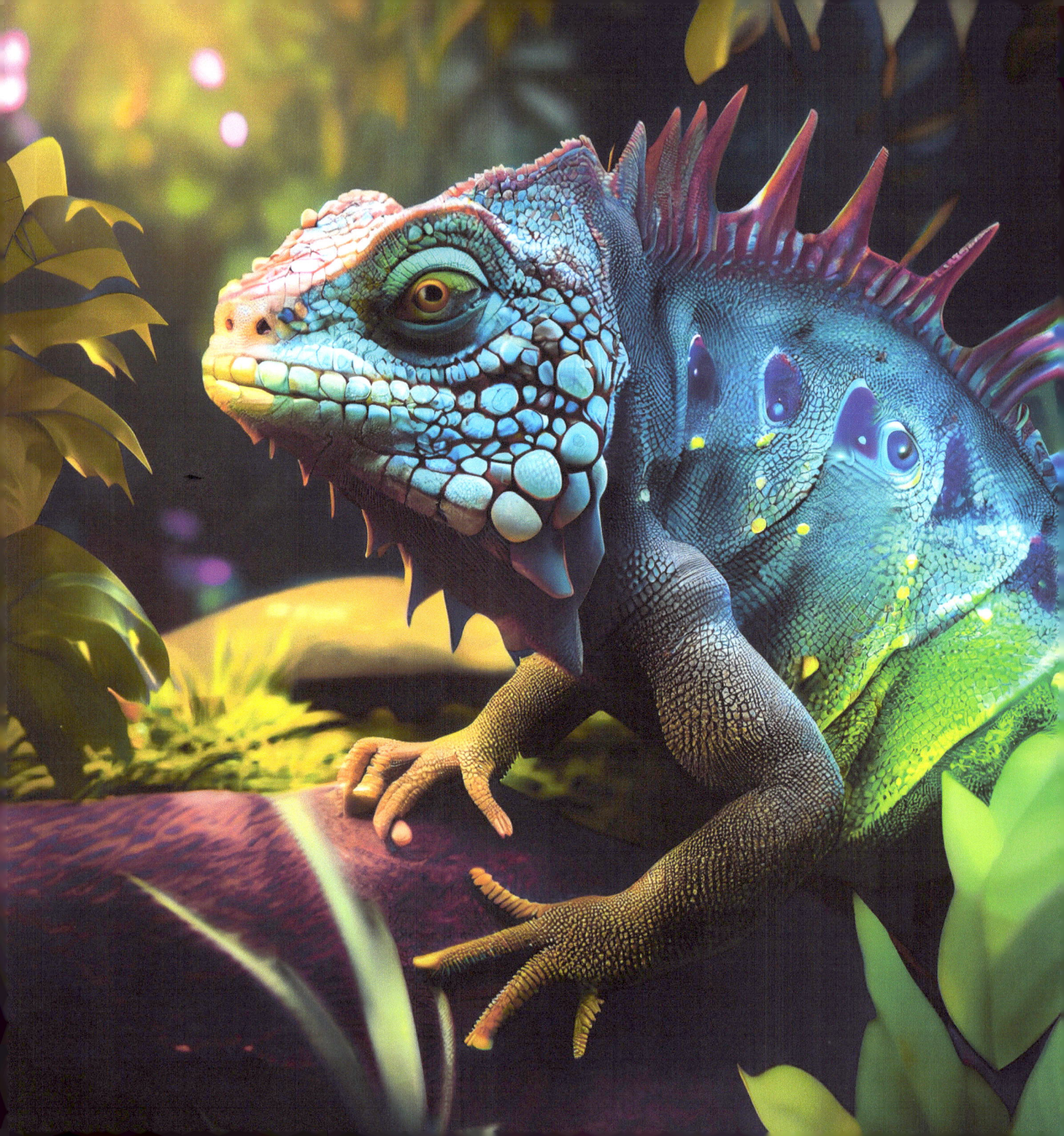

Isla the Iguana

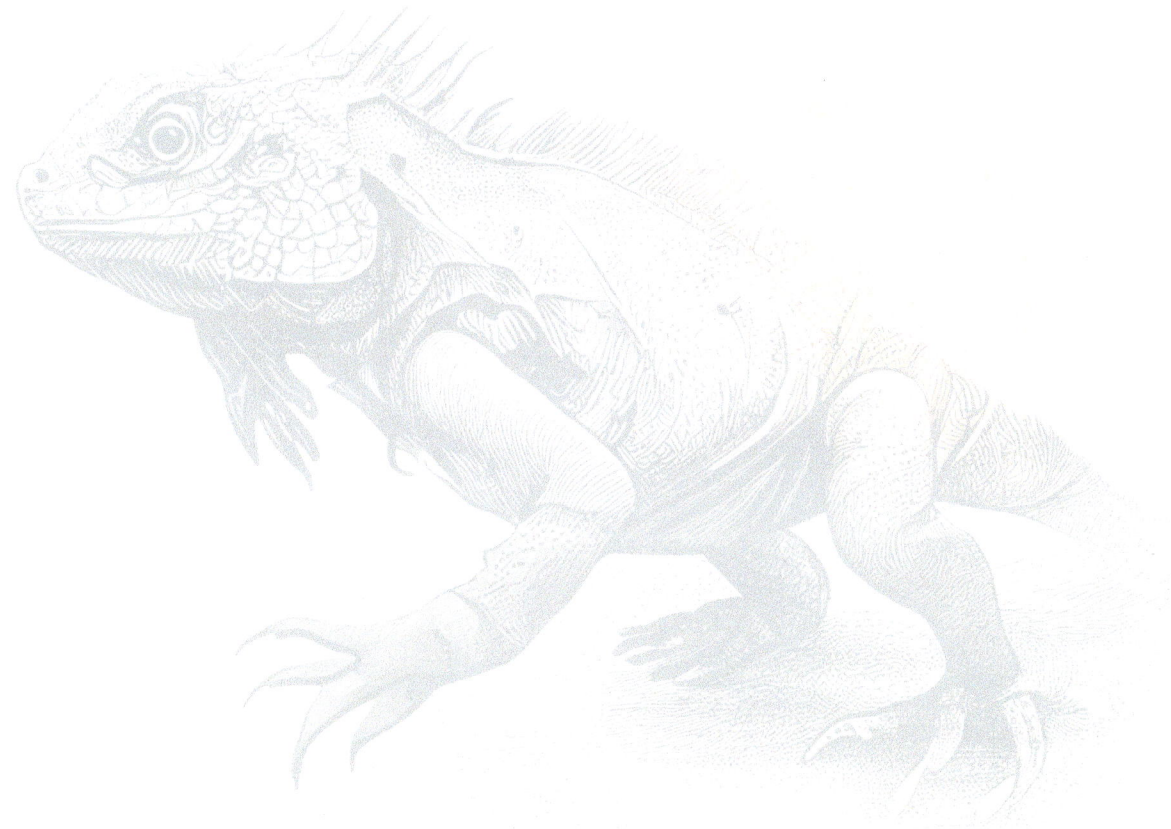

like to bask in the sun

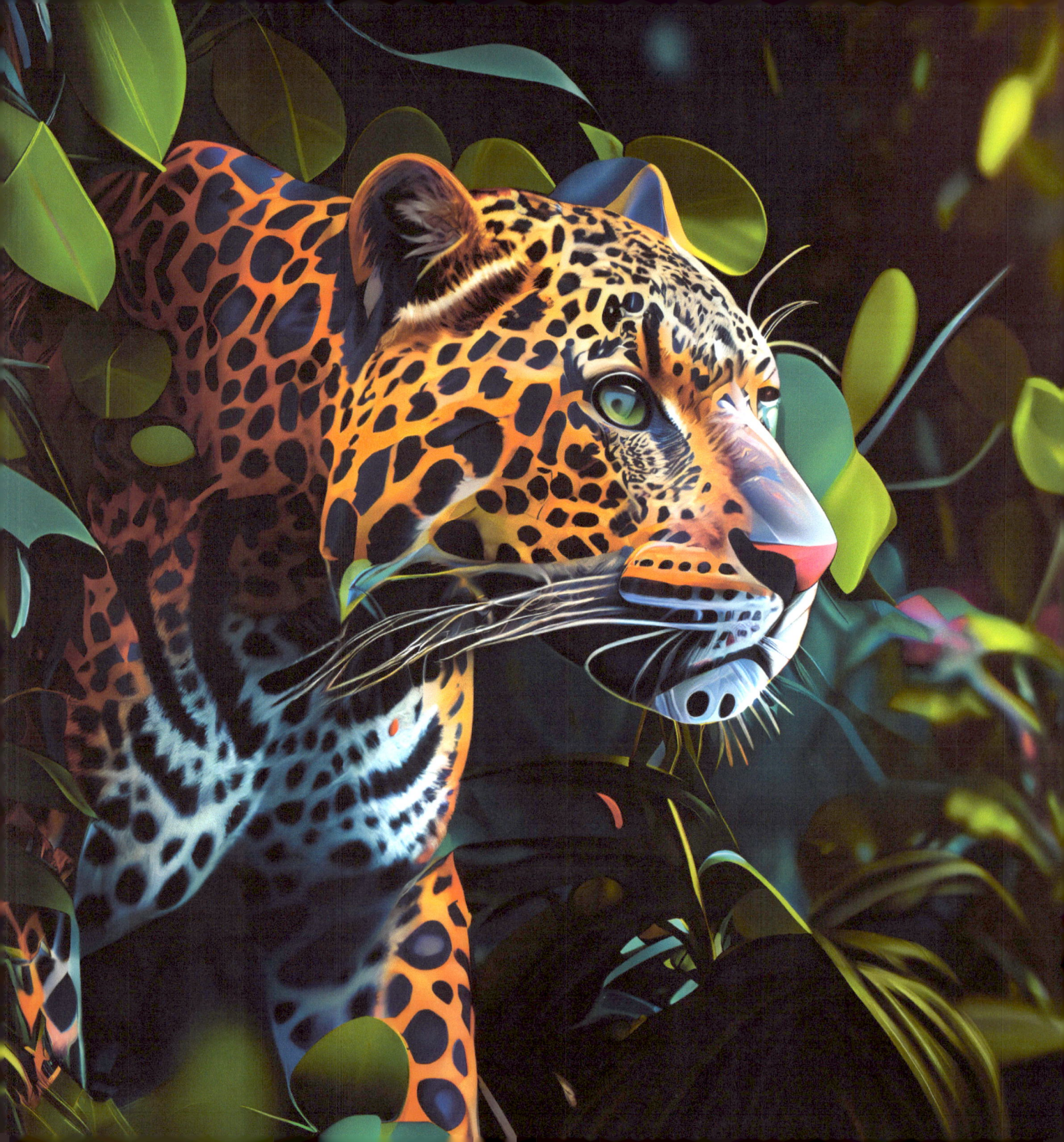

Jerry the Jaguar

ran fast and had fun

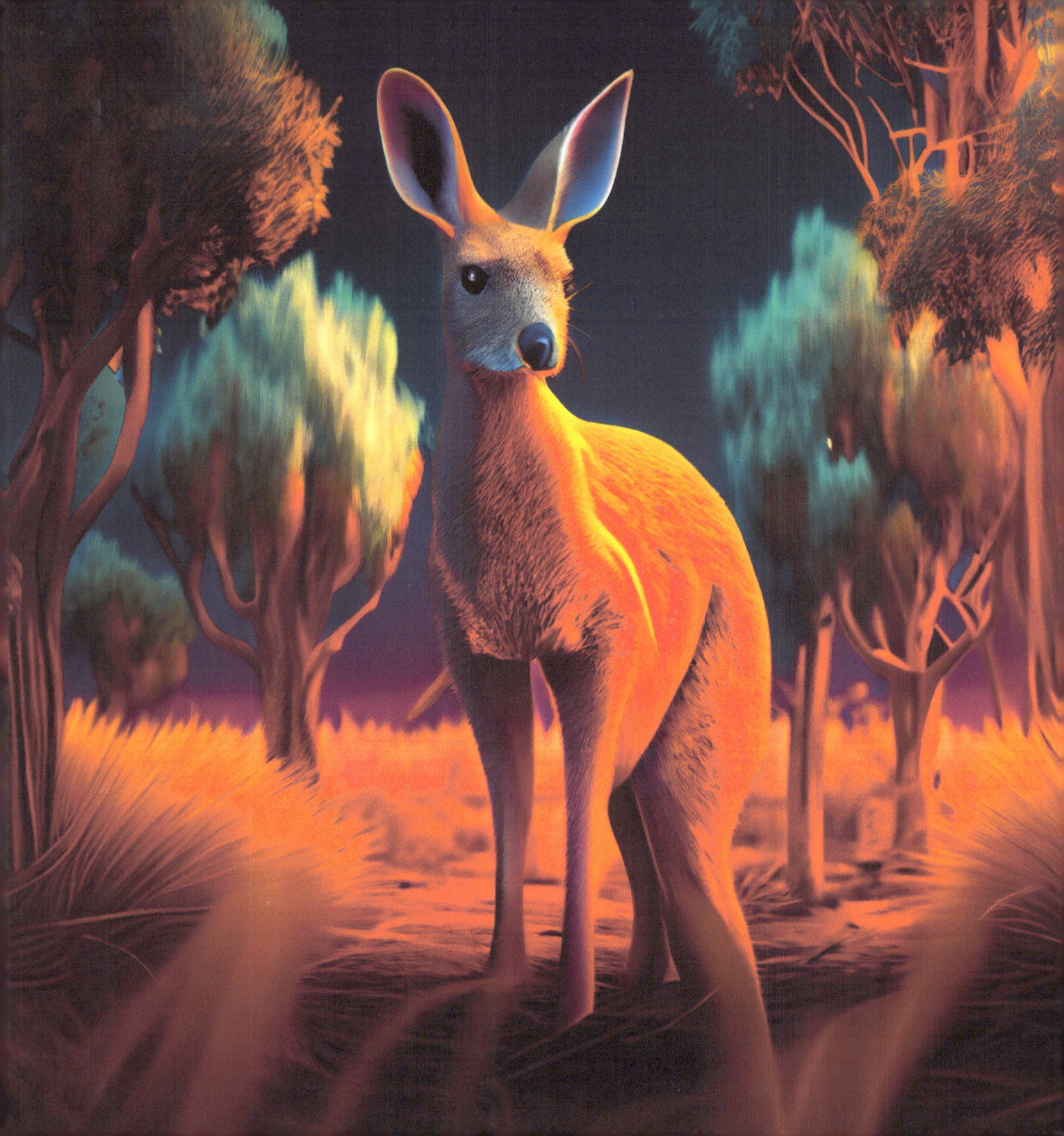

Katie the Kangaroo

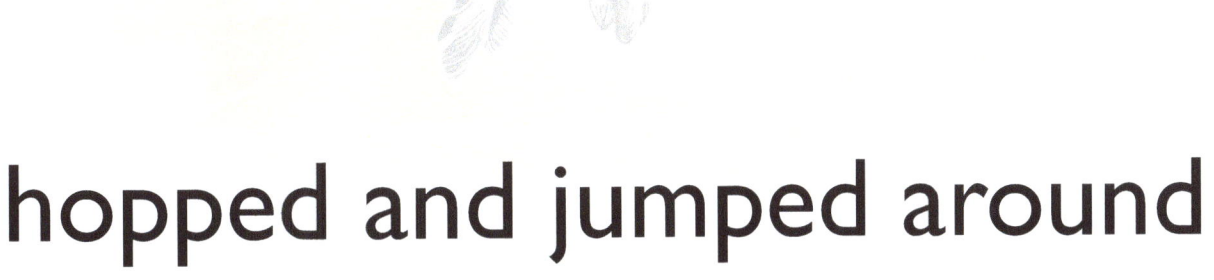

hopped and jumped around

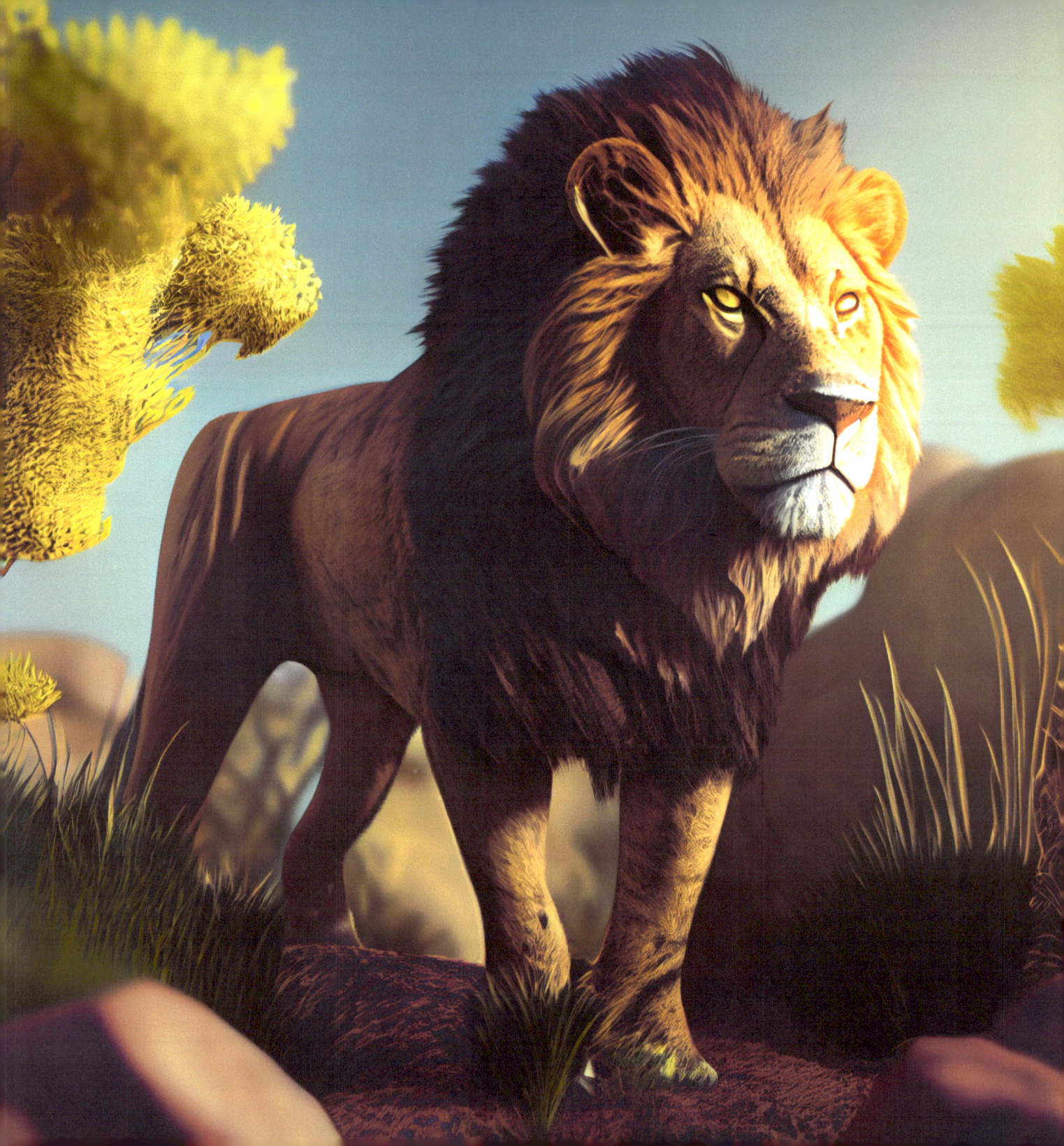

Leo the Lion

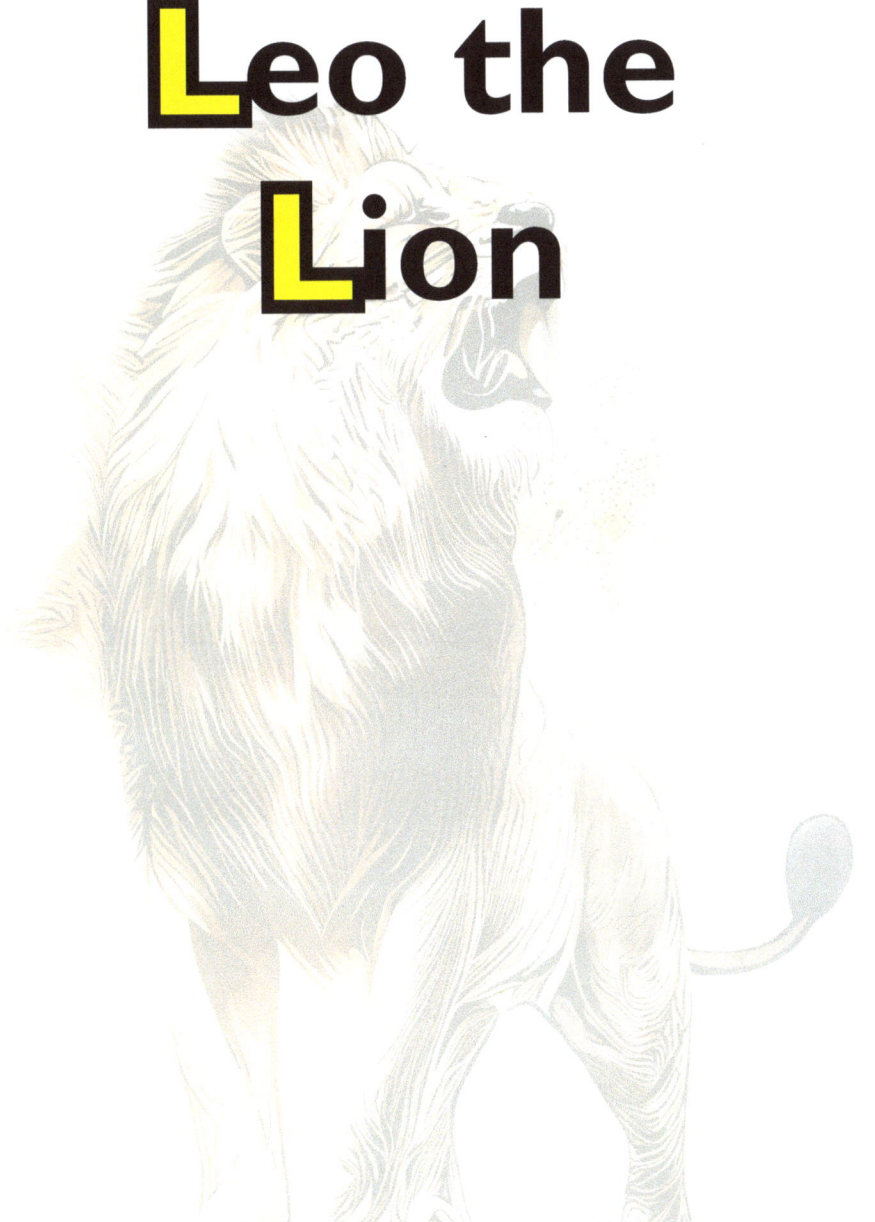

roared with a mighty sound

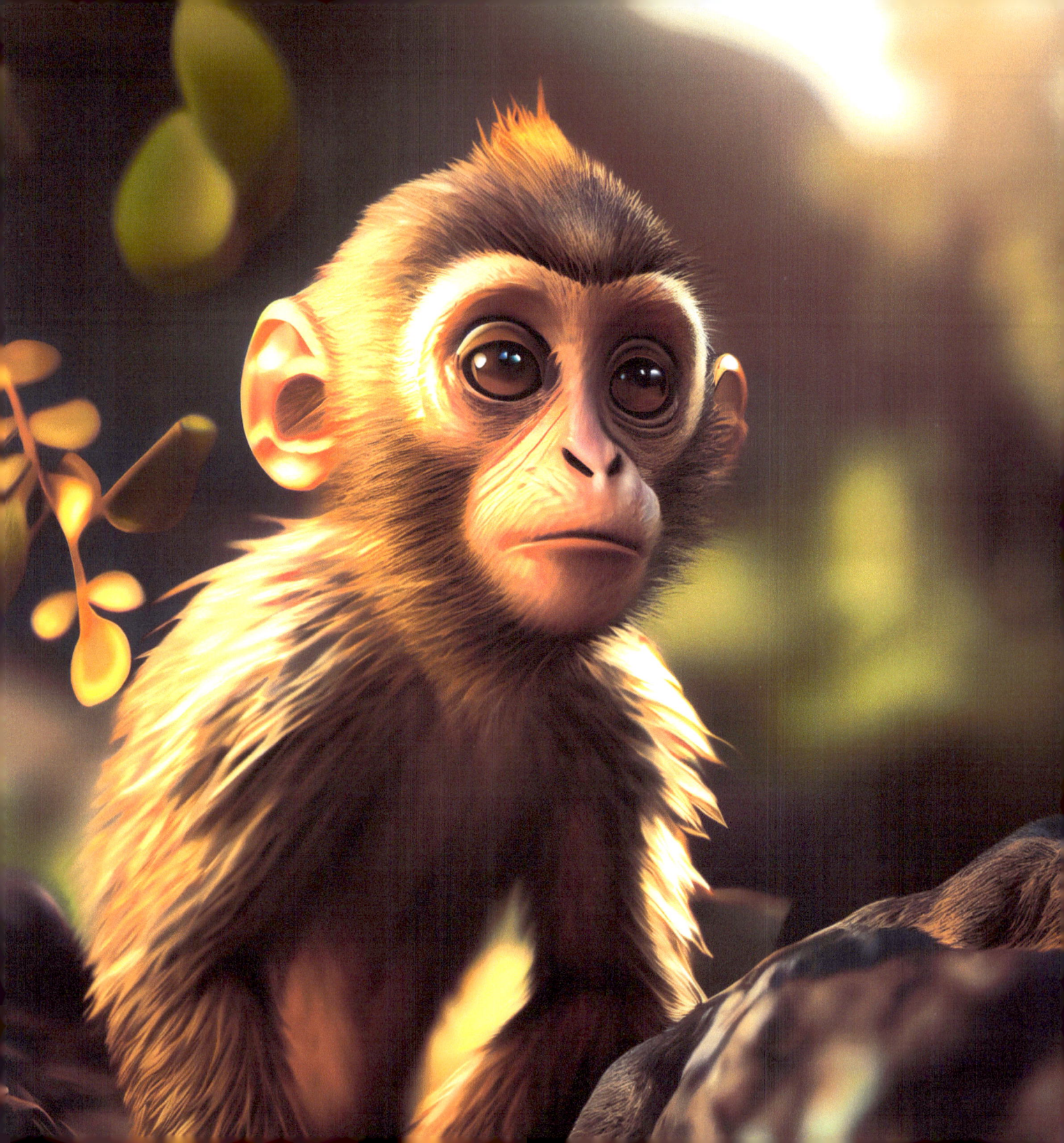

Mia the Monkey

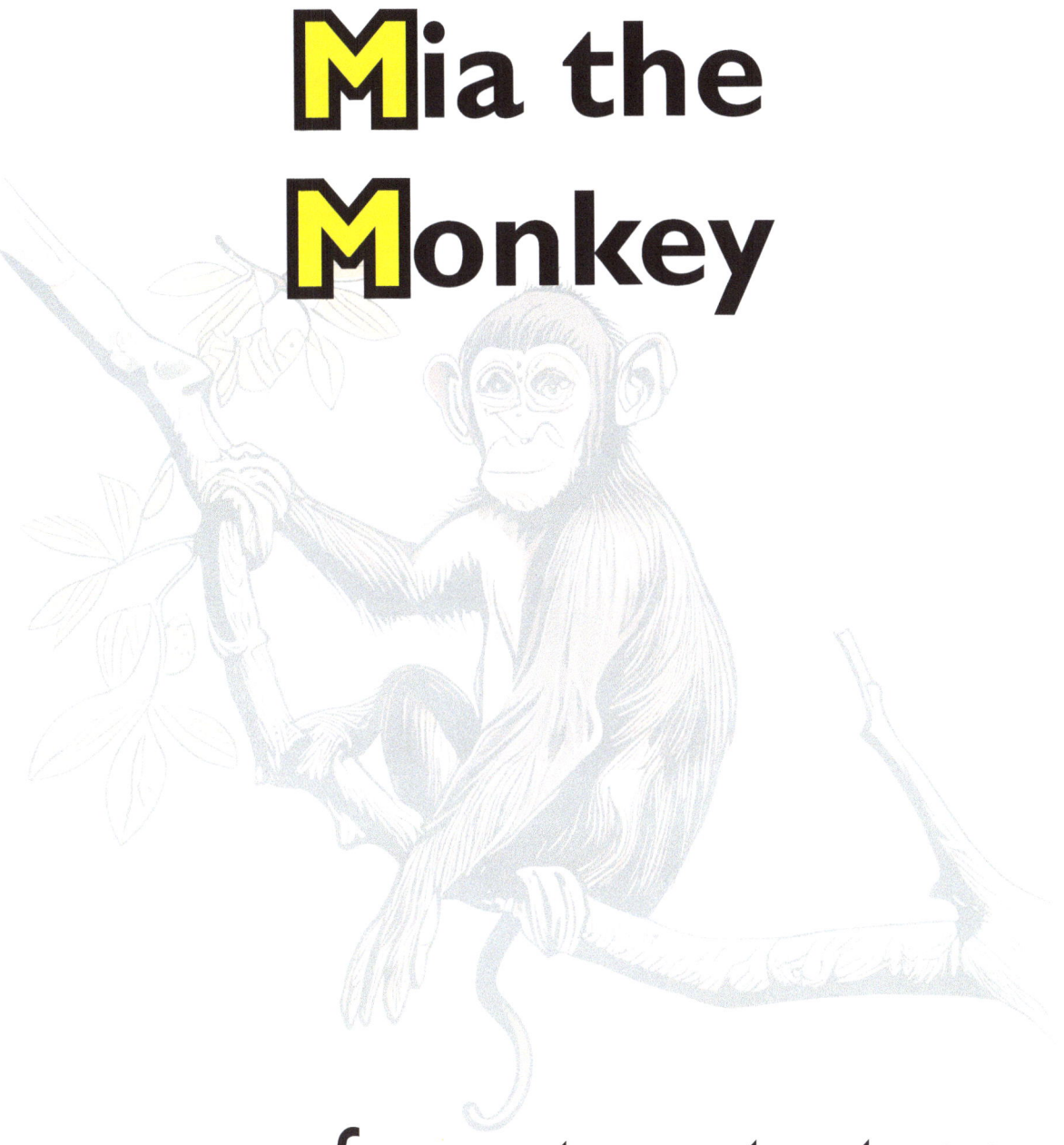

swung from tree to tree

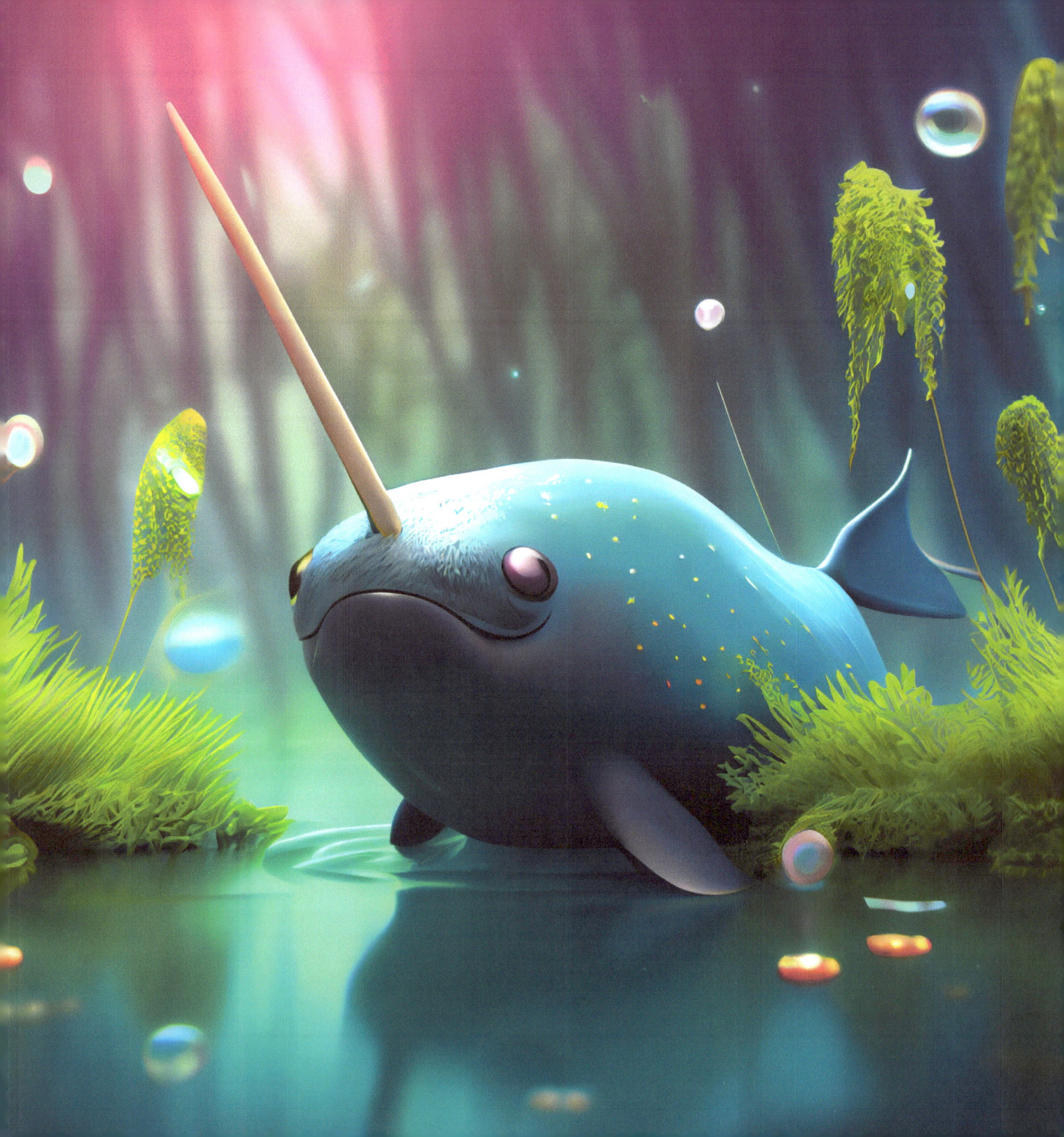

Nora the Narwhal

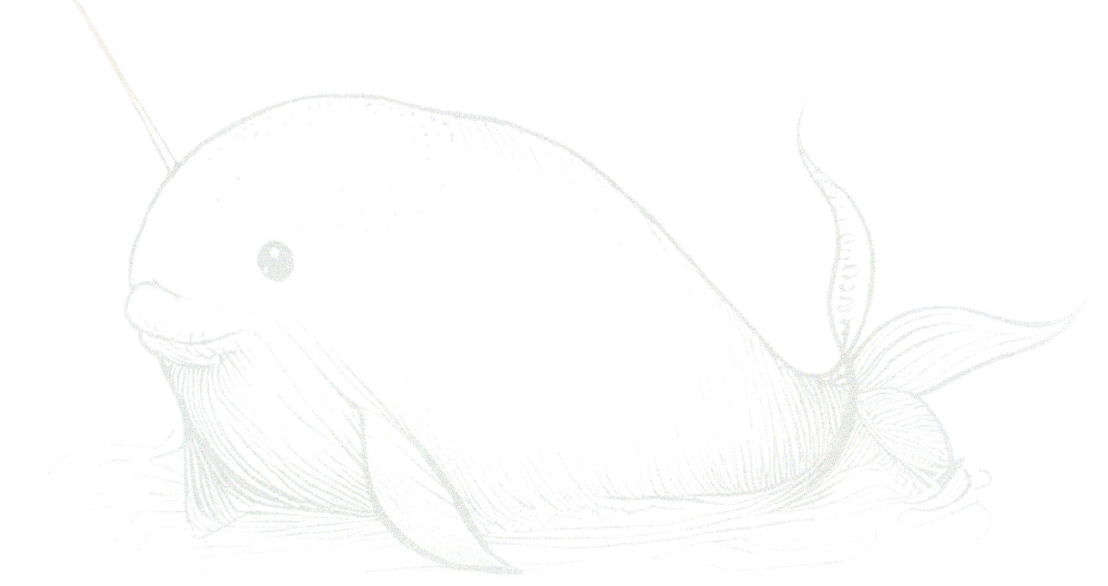

swam in the deep sea

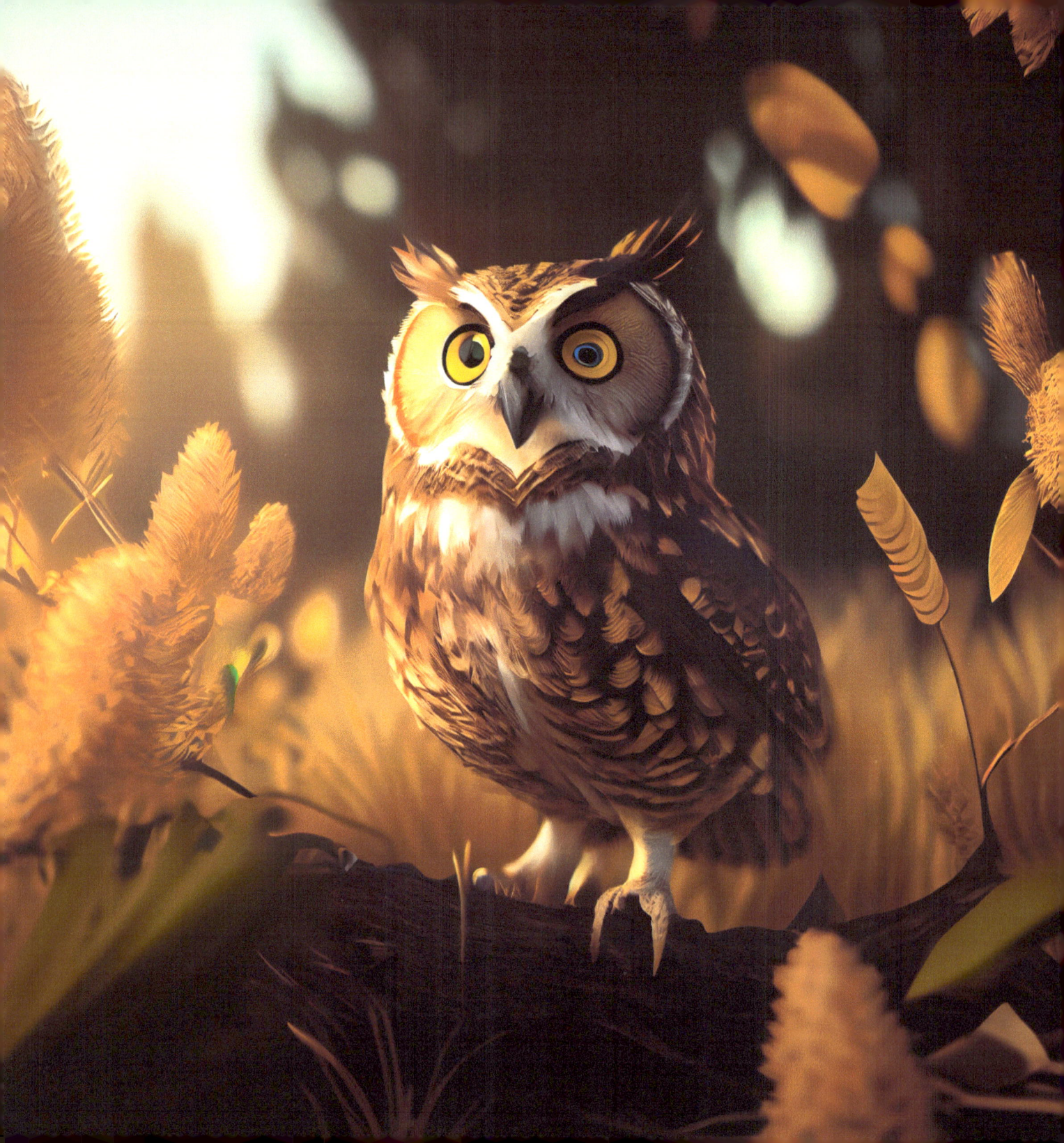

Olivia the Owl

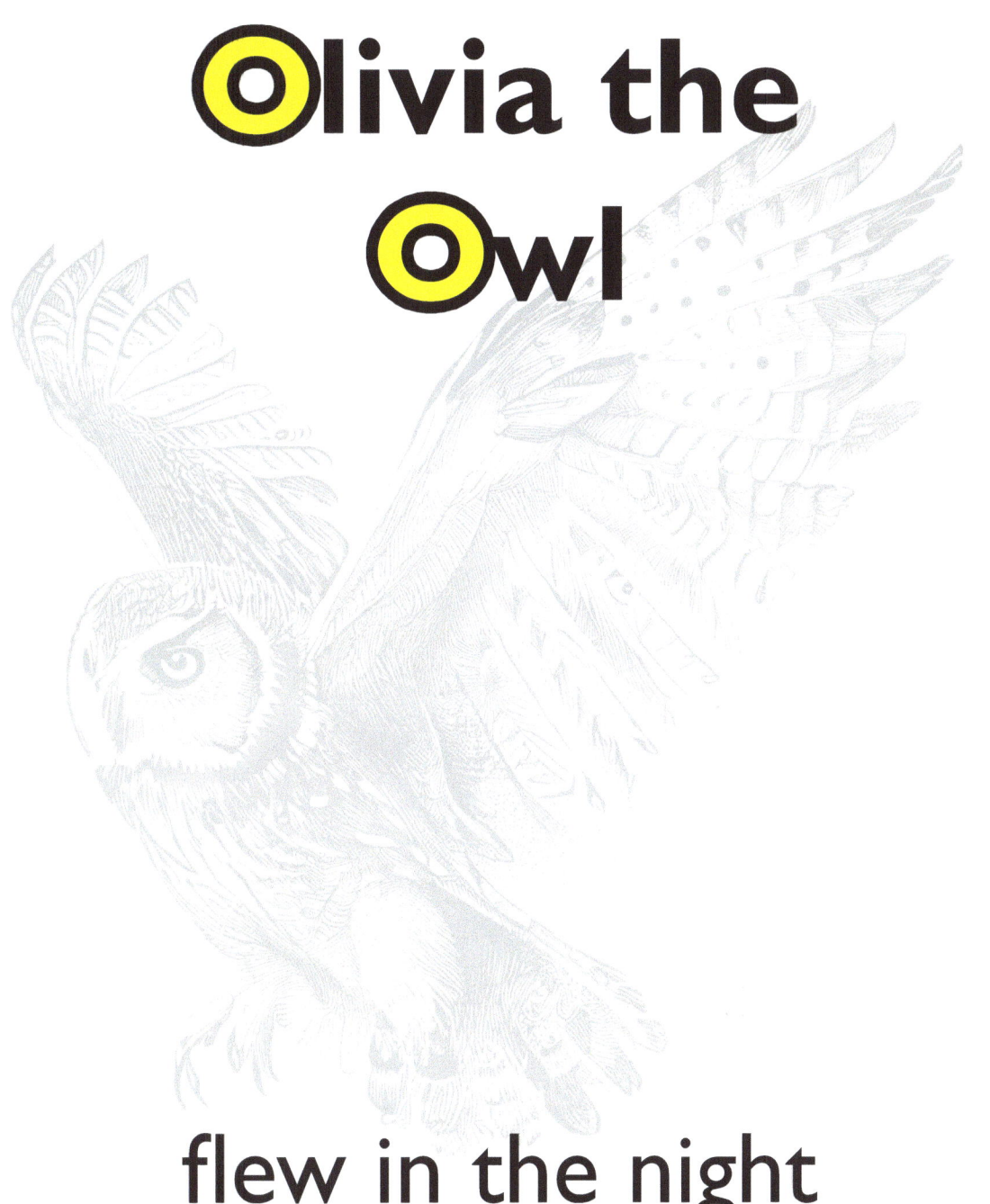

flew in the night

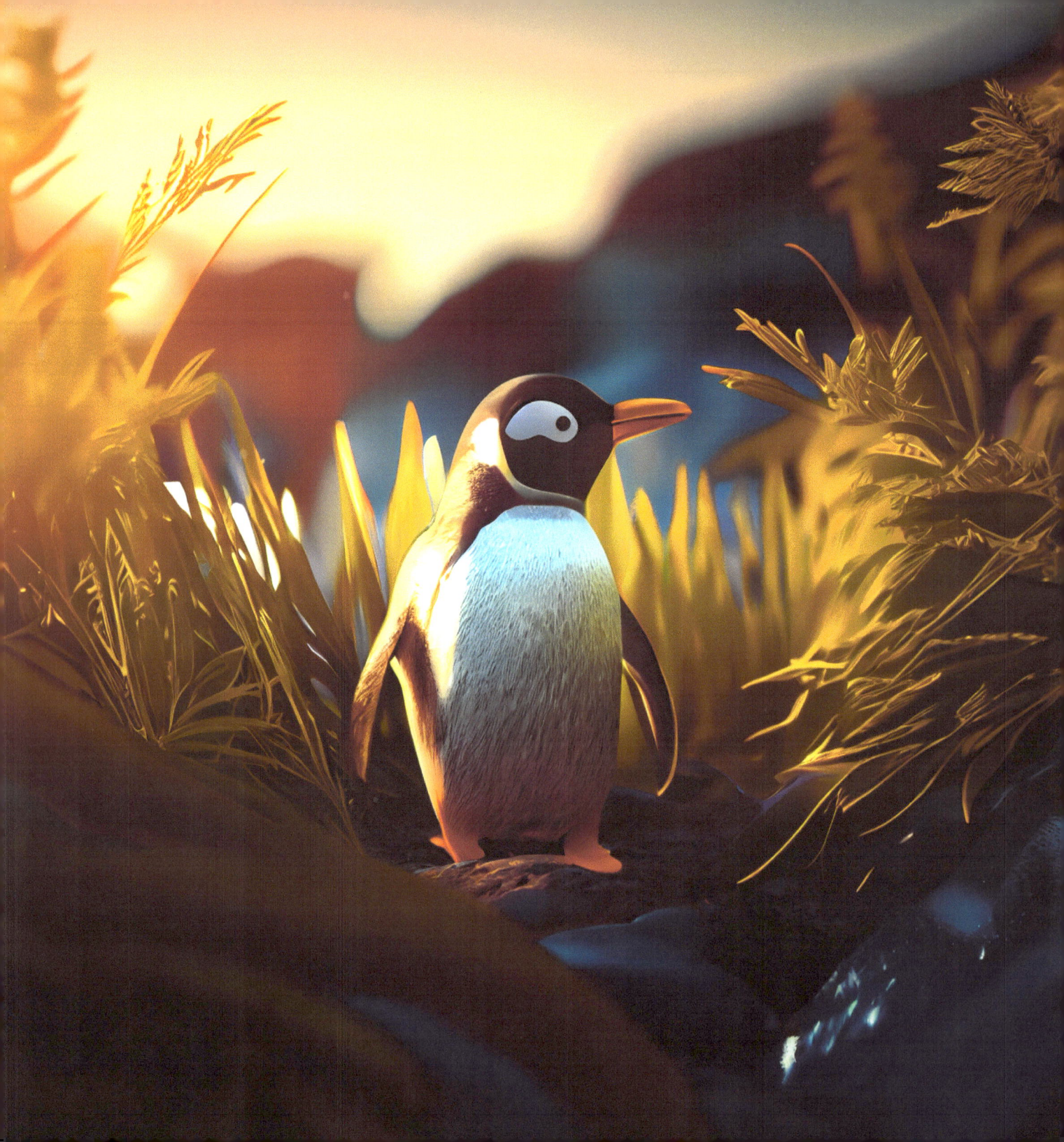

Pete the
Penguin

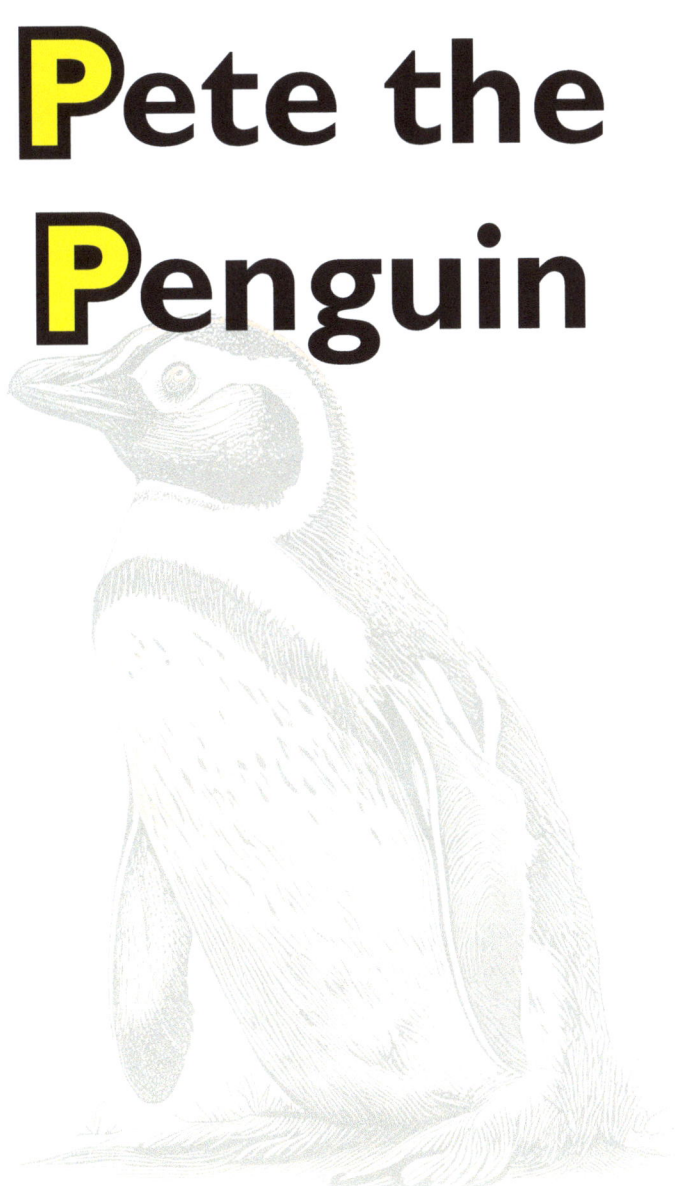

waddled with delight

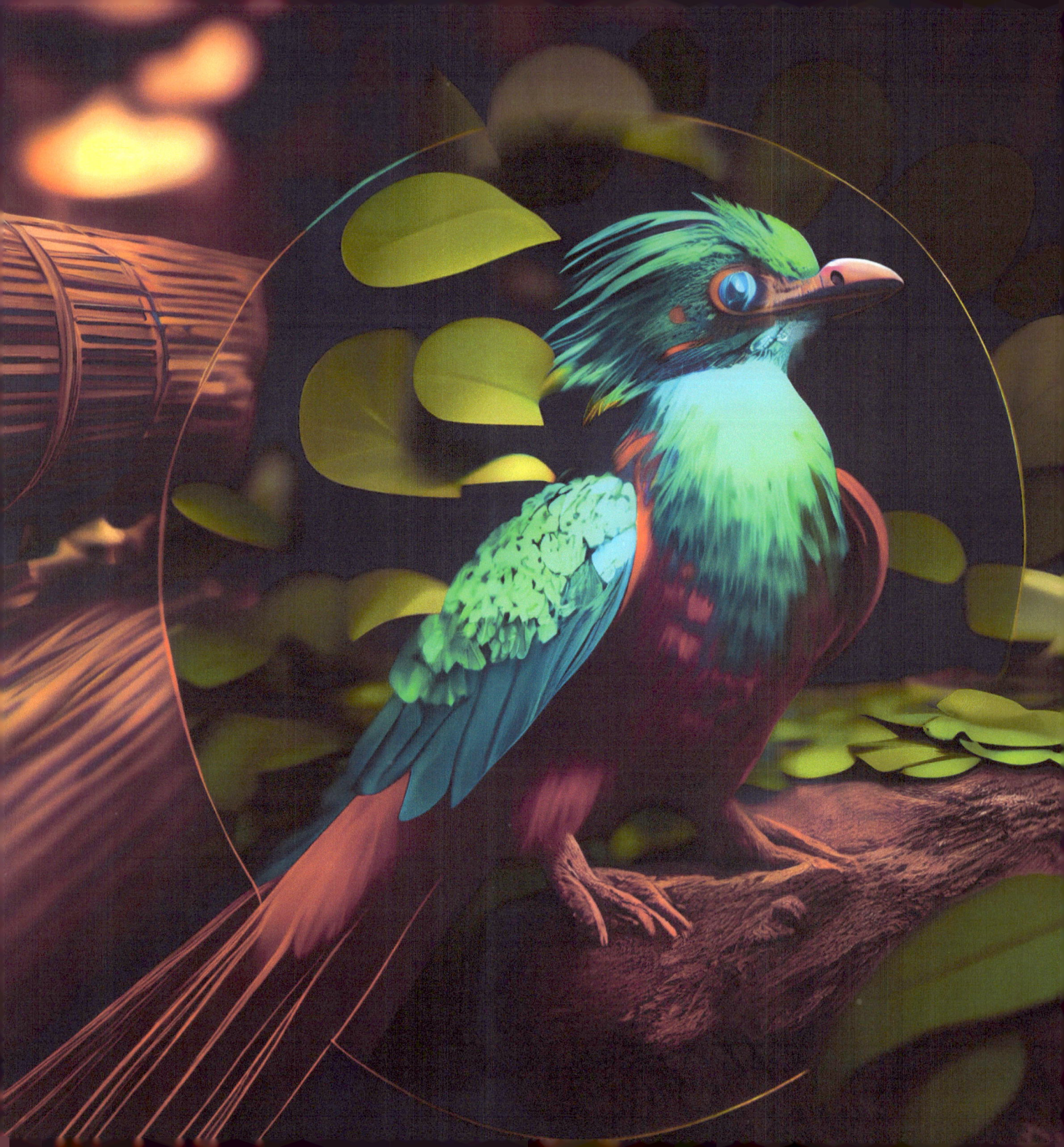

Quincy the Quetzal

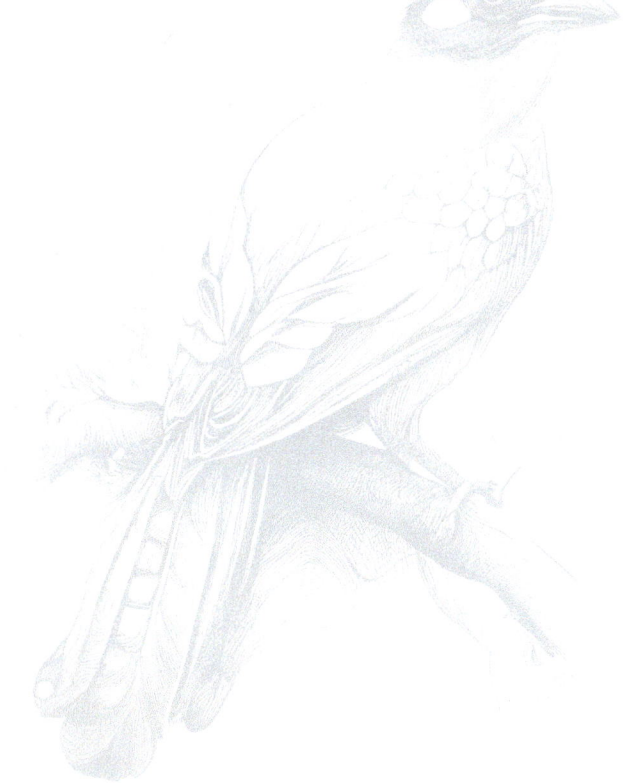

was brightly colored and rare

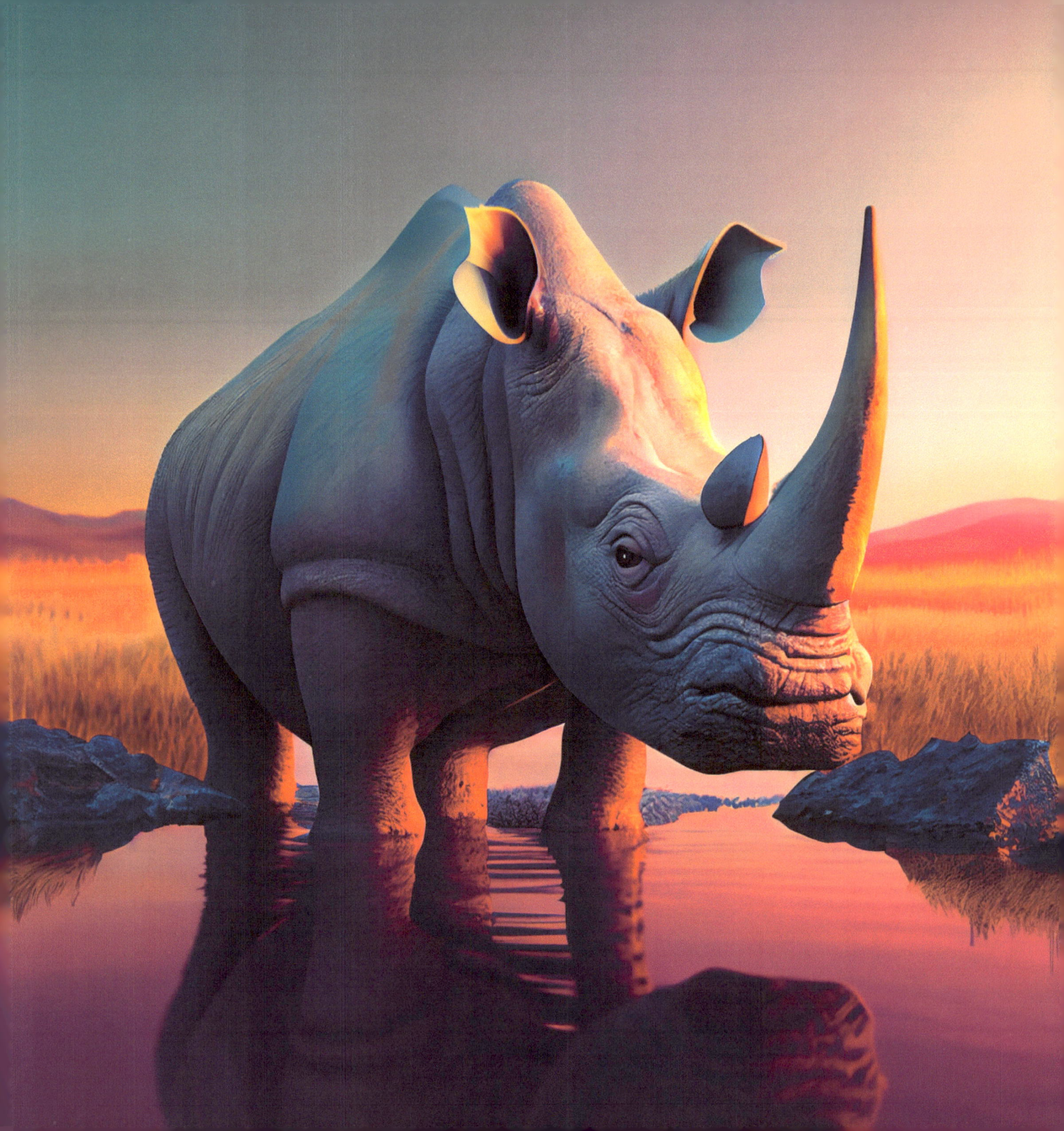

Rocky the Rhino

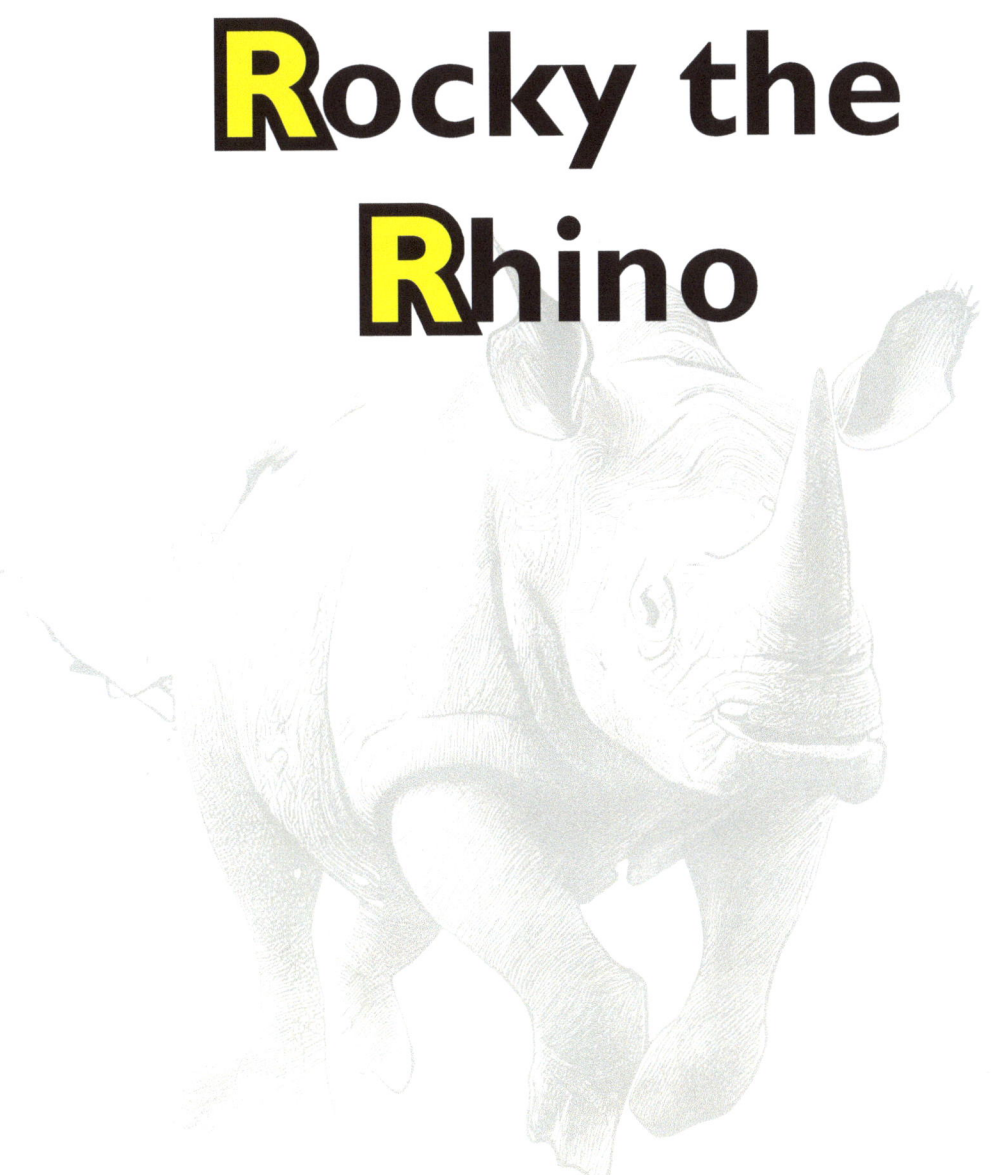

stood strong and square

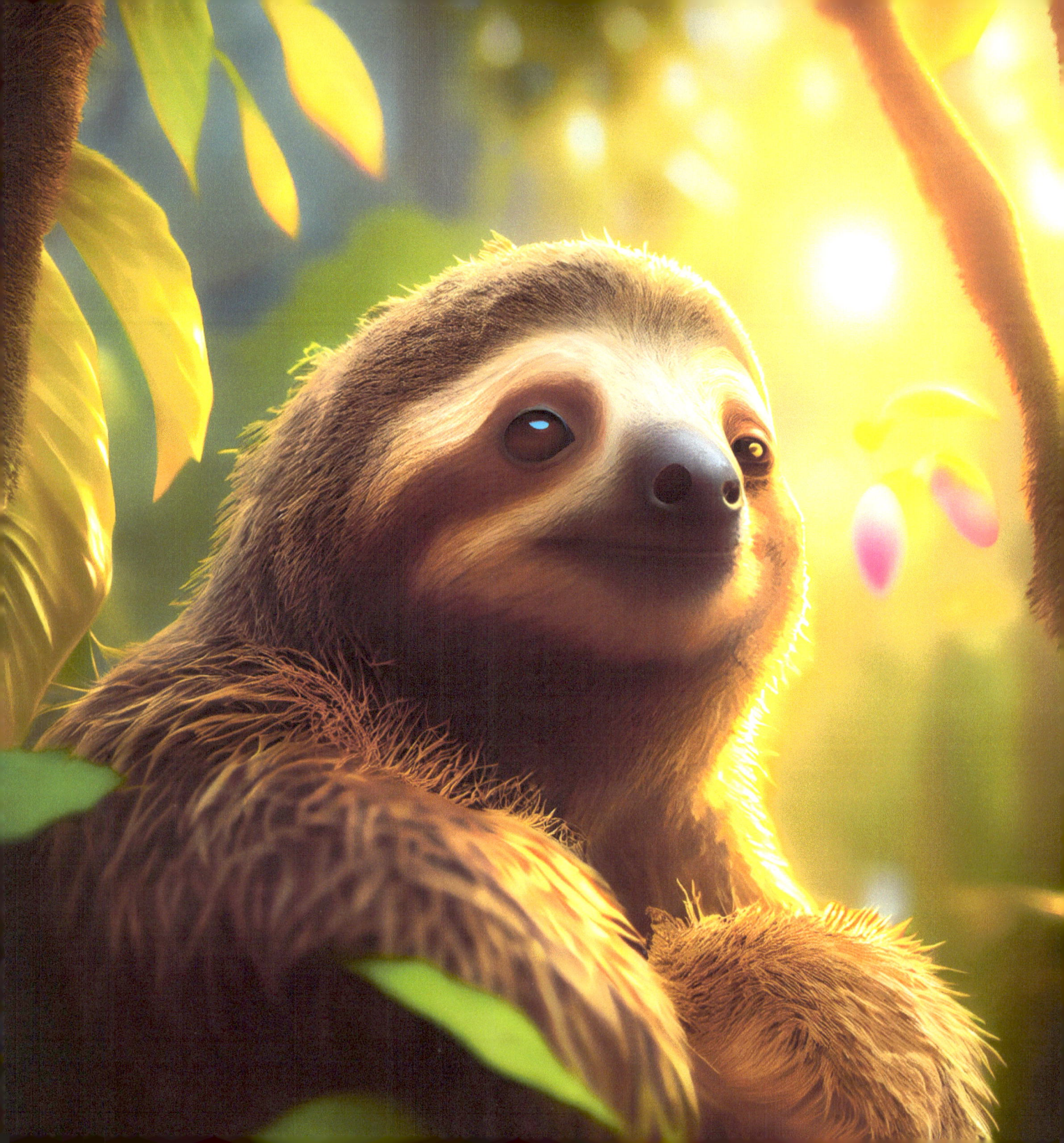

Sophie the Sloth

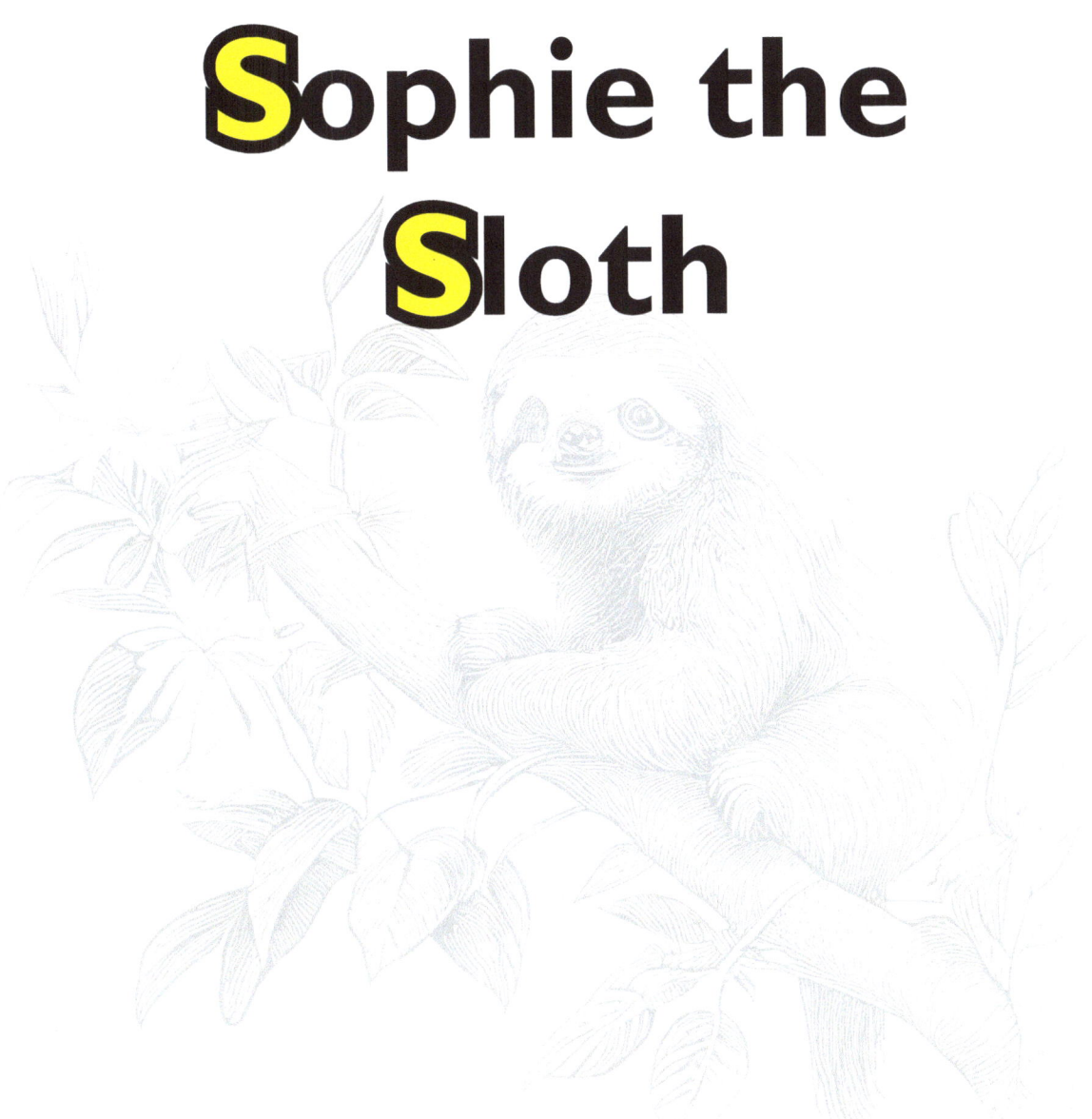

was slow but very sweet

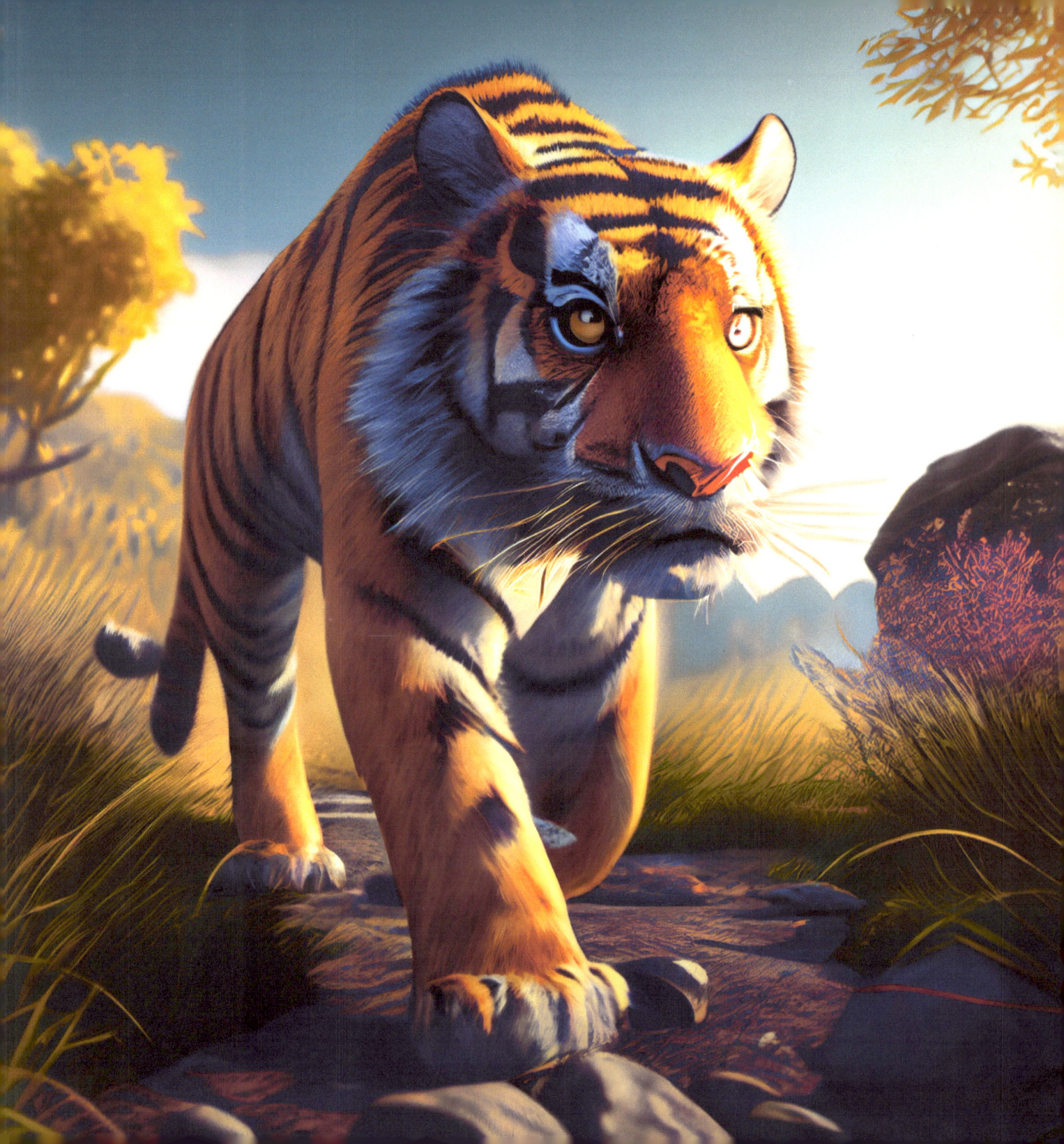

Timmy the Tiger

had big strong feet

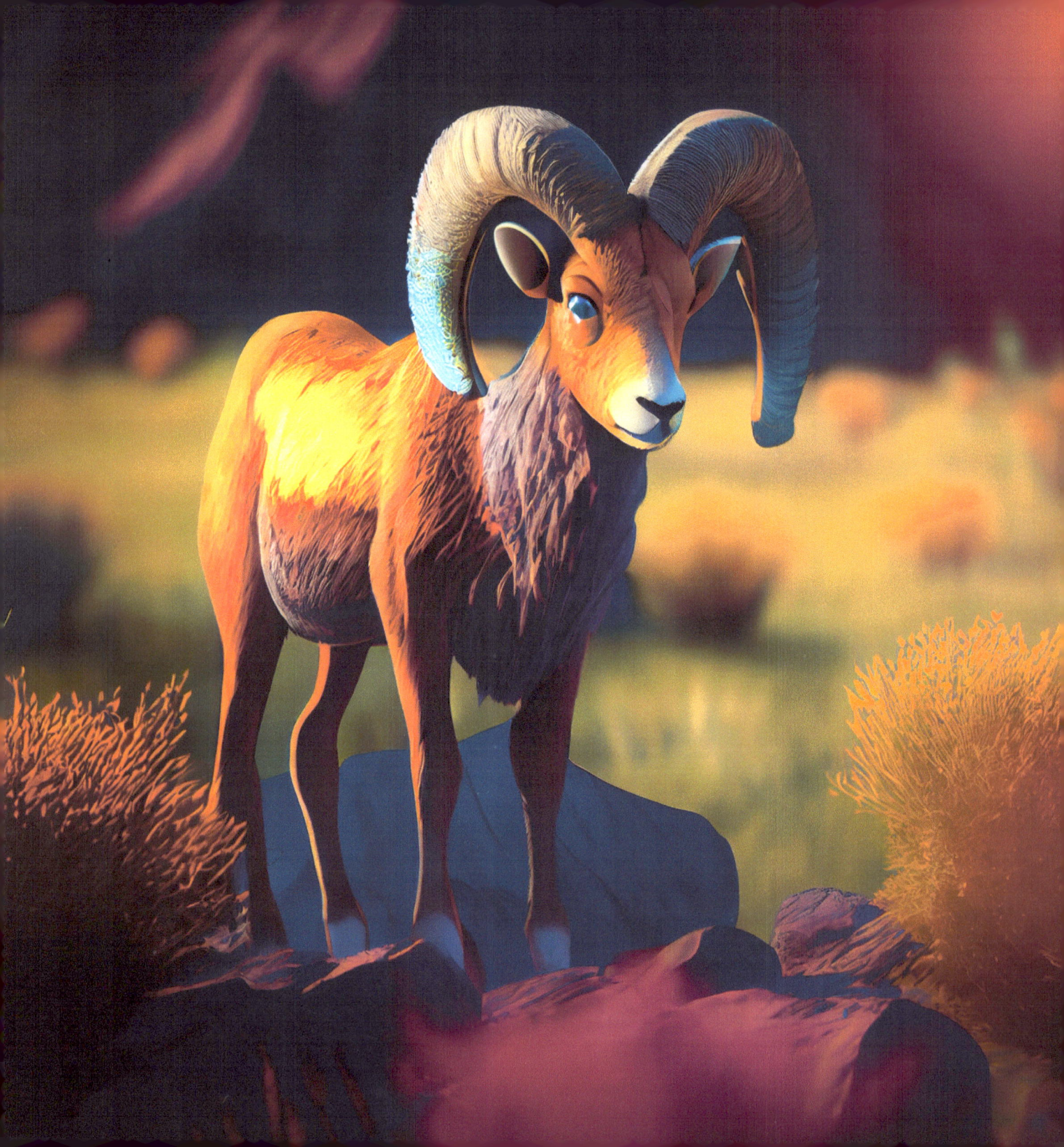

Uma the Urial

was a mountain goat

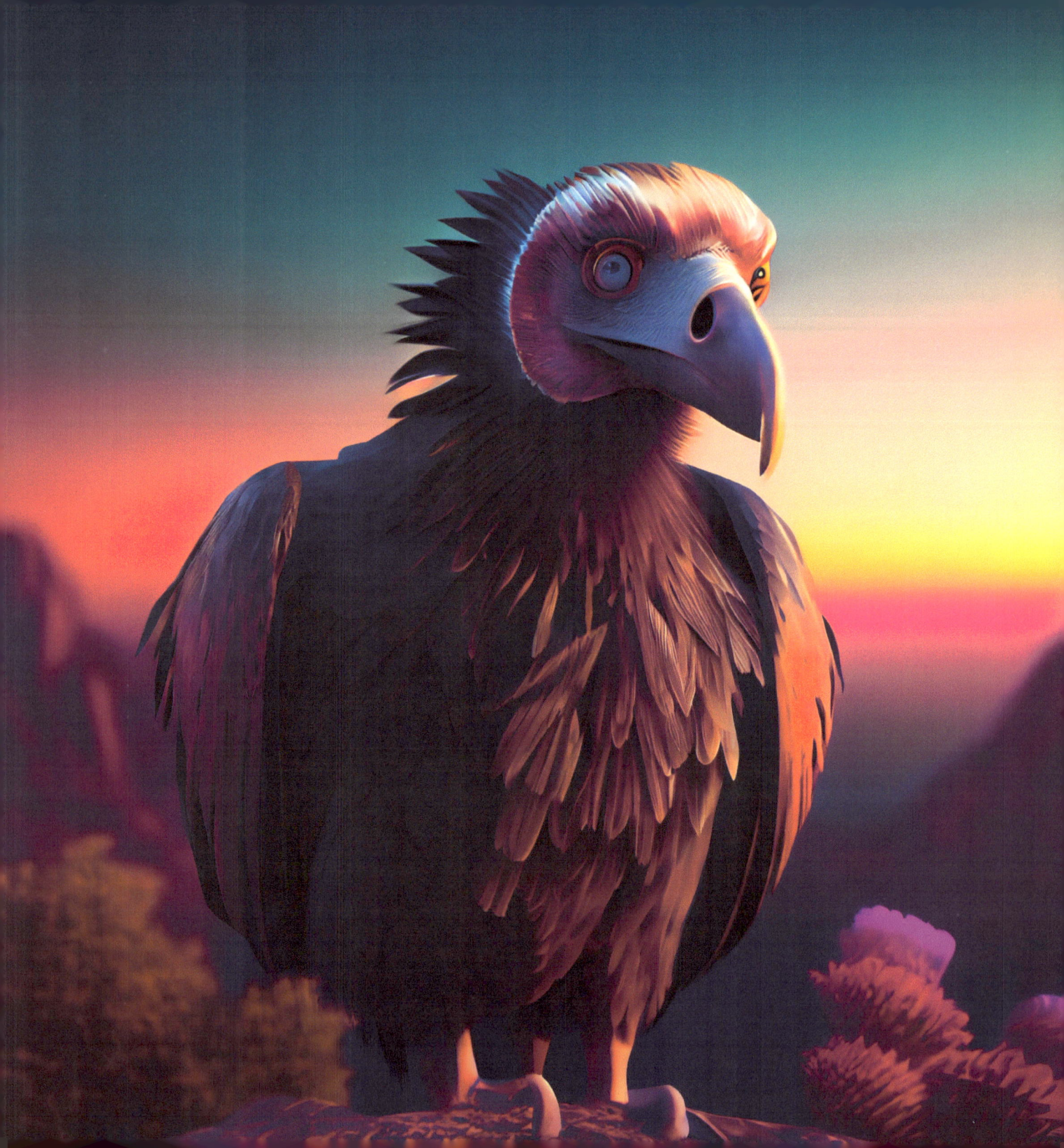

Vera the
Vulture

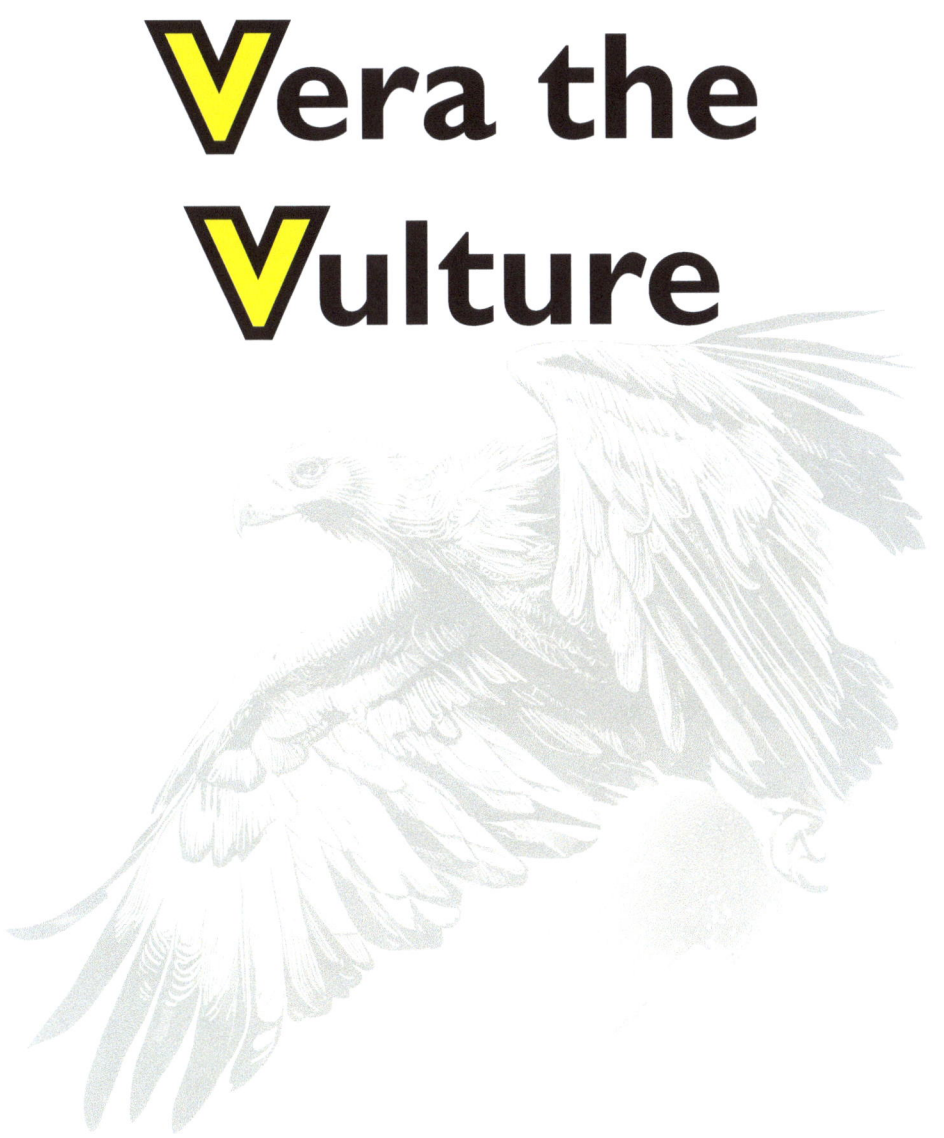

soared and could float

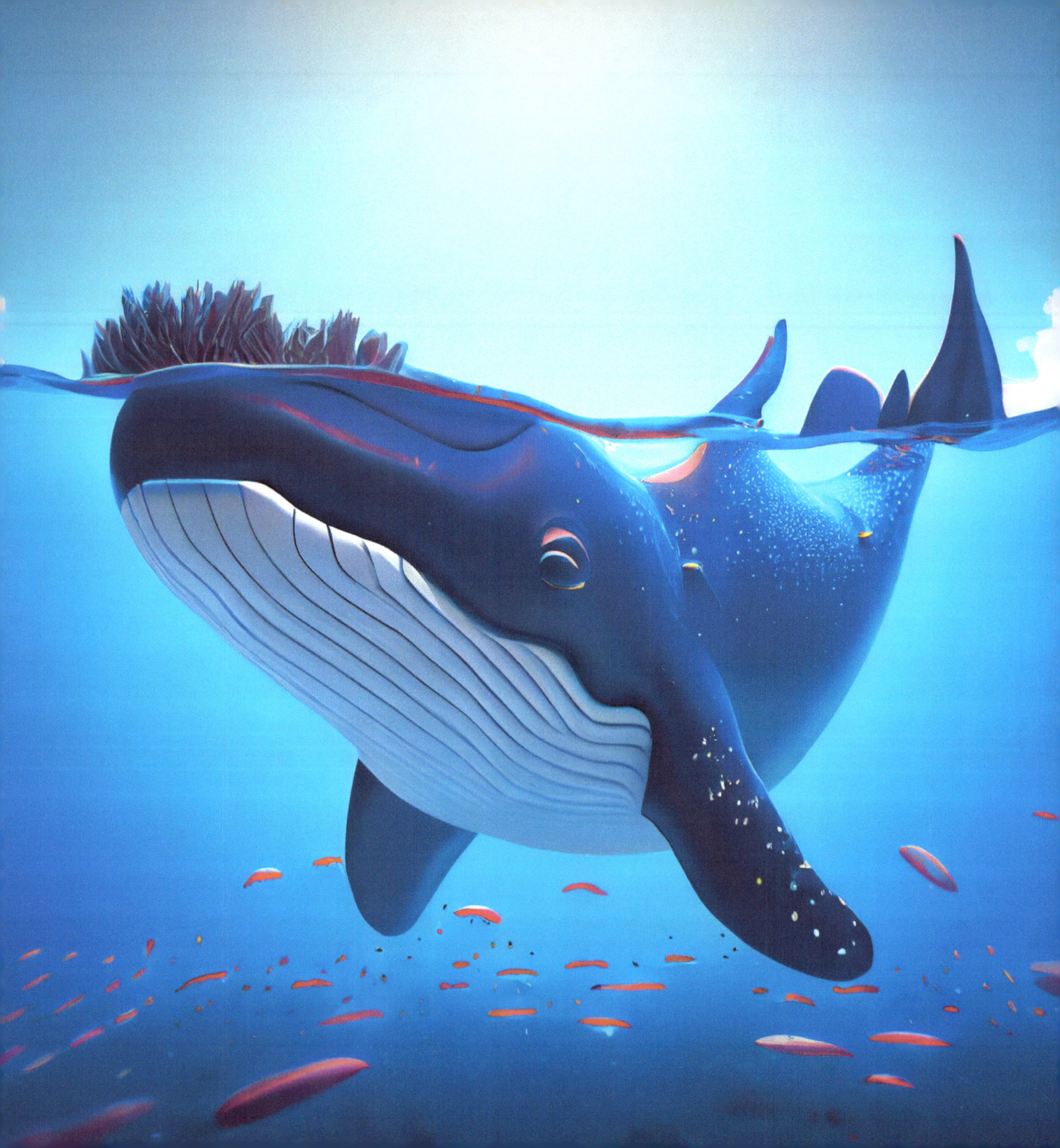

Wendy the Whale

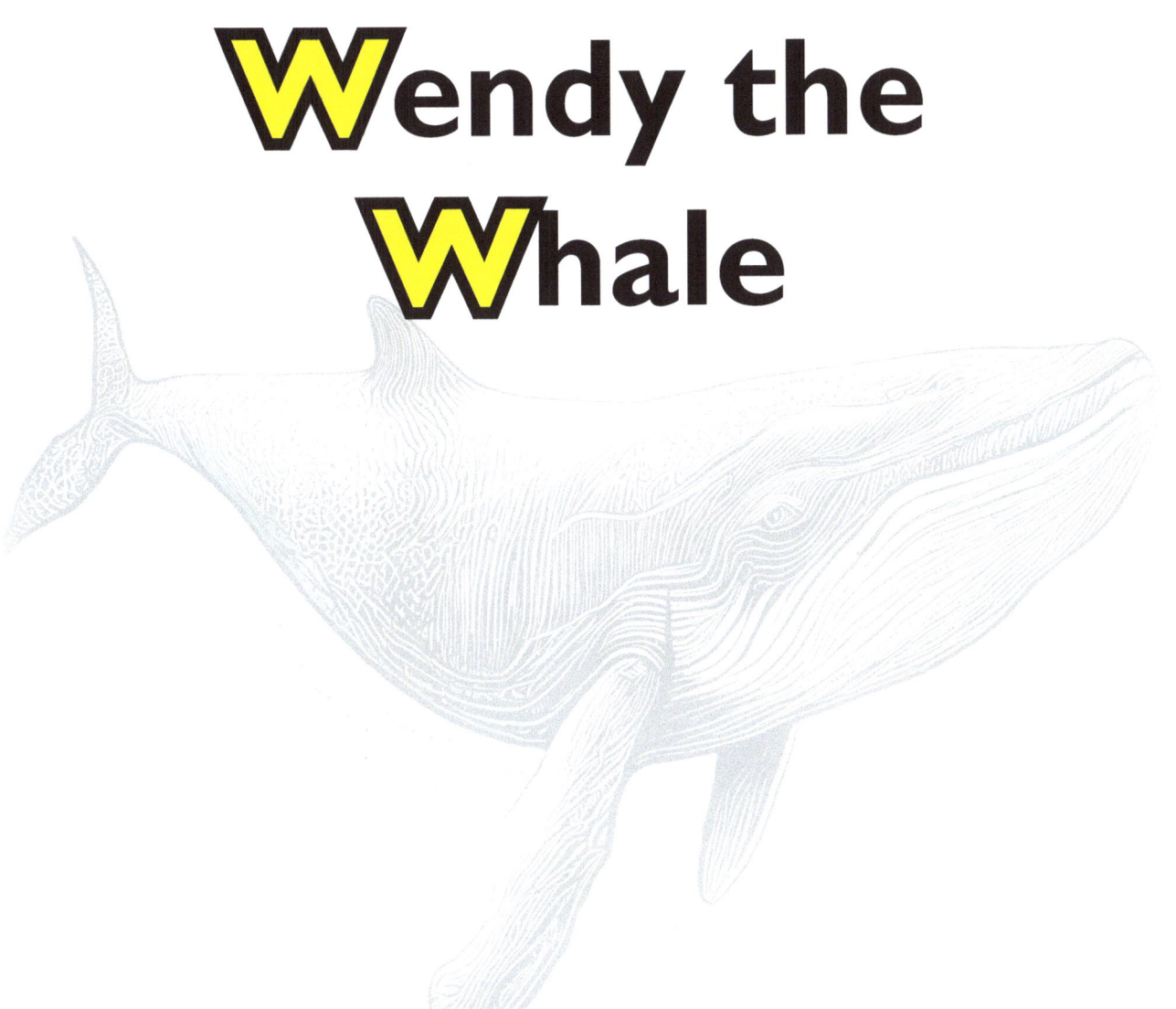

swam in the ocean blue

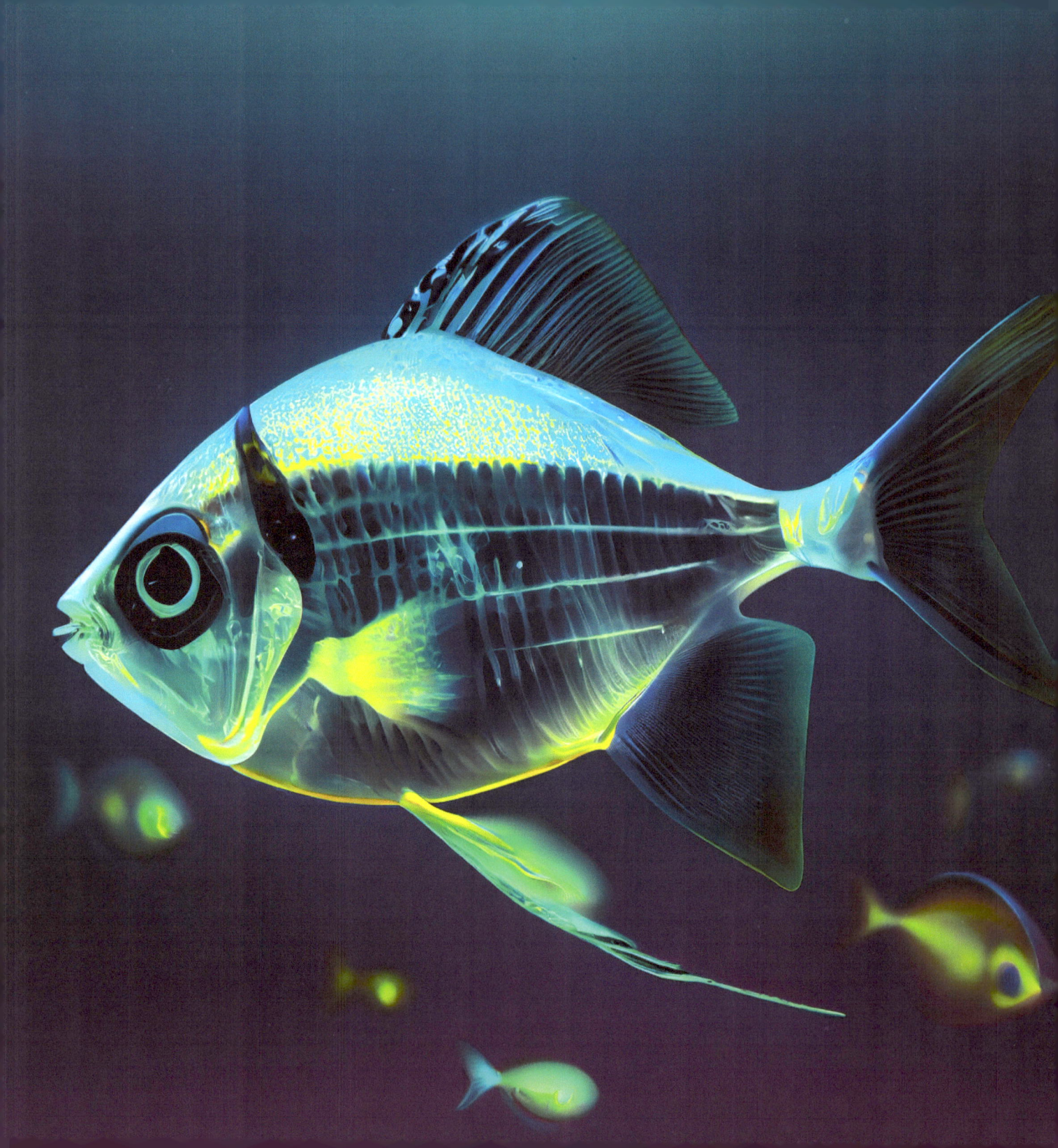

Xander the Xray Tetra

had a room with a view

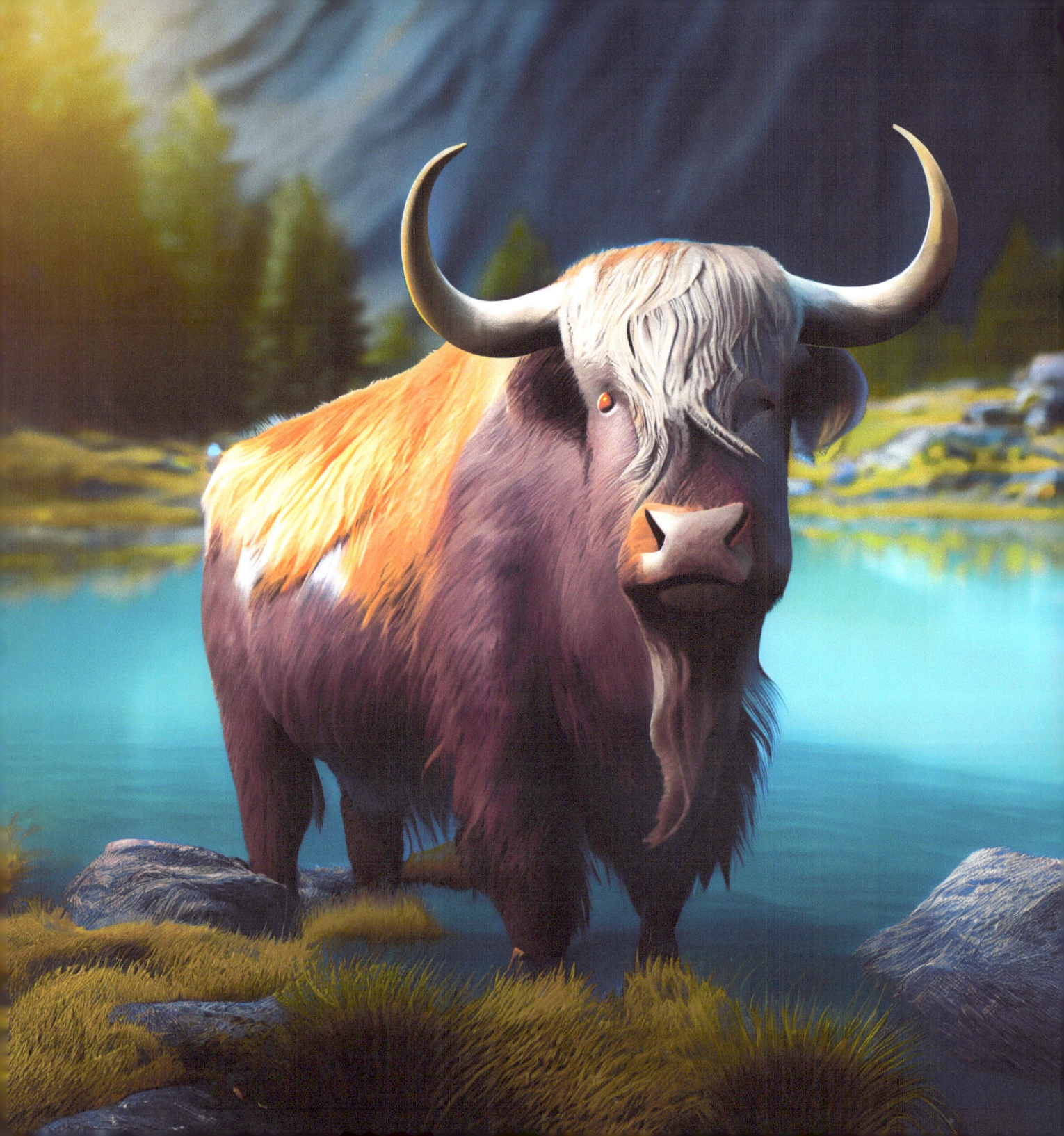

Yara the Yak

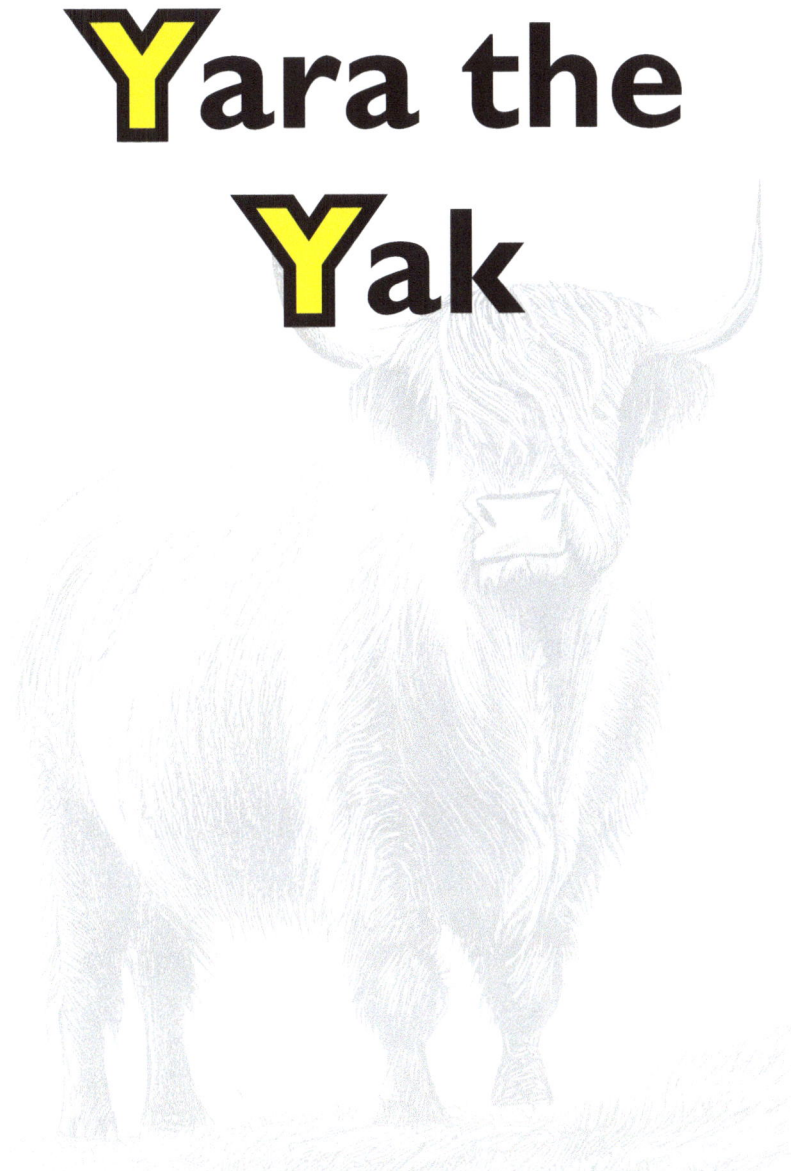

had fur that was thick

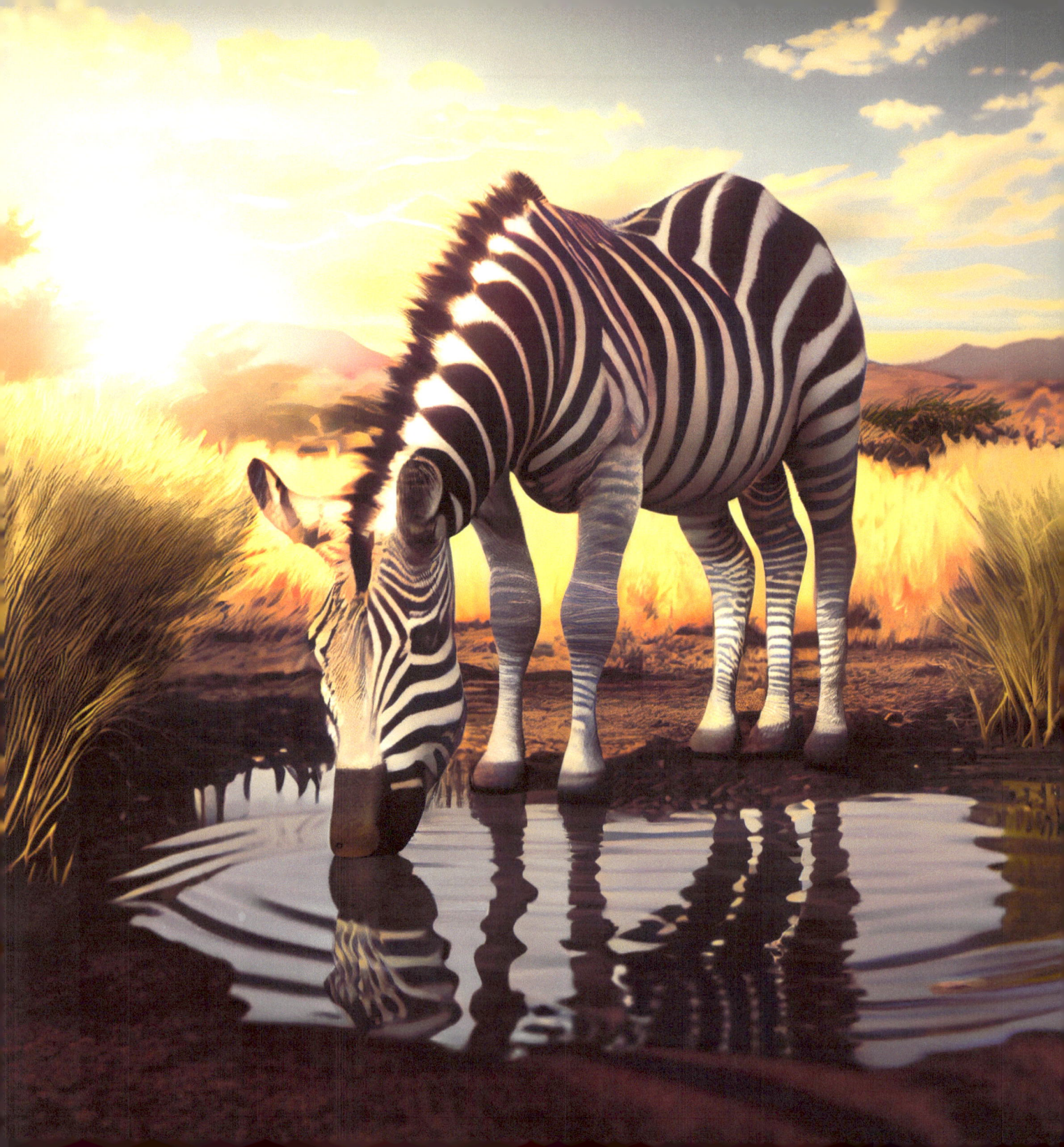

Zane the Zebra

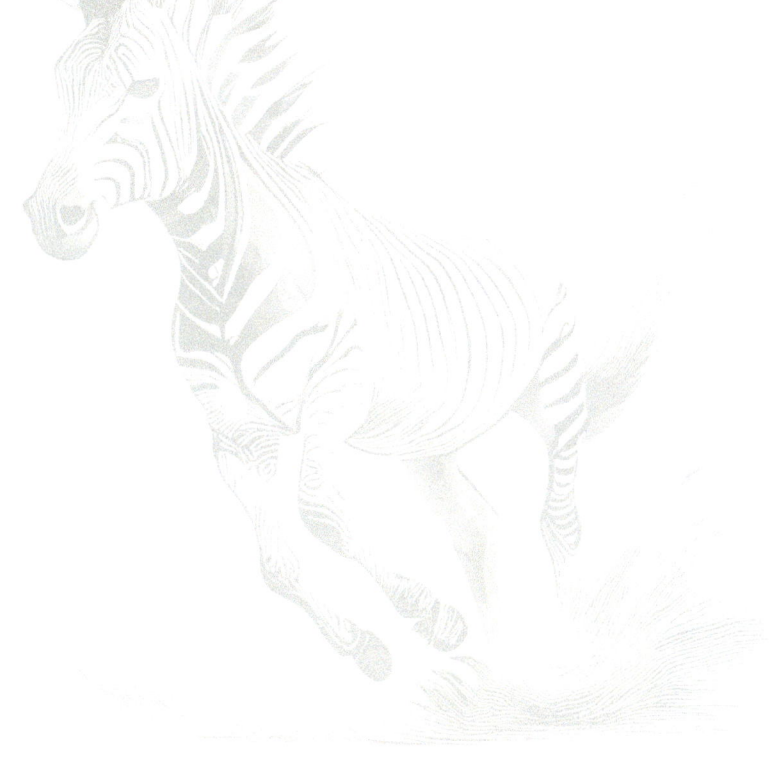

could run very quick